The Royal Court Theatre presents
The Abbey Theatre production of

THE *cavalcaders*

by Billy Roche

First performance at the Peacock Theatre,
Dublin on 14 July 1993

First performance at the Royal Court Theatre
on 6 January 1994

*Financially assisted by the Royal Borough of Kensington and Chelsea
Recipient of an Arts Council Incentive Funding Award*

*Recipient of a grant from the Theatre Restoration Fund &
from the Foundation for Sports & the Arts*

*The Royal Court's Play Development Programme is
funded by the Audrey Skirball-Kenis Theatre*

Registered Charity number 231242

THE ENGLISH STAGE COMPANY

The English Stage Company was formed to bring serious writing back to the stage. The Court's first Artistic Director, George Devine, wanted to create a vital and popular theatre. In order to promote this, he encouraged new writing that explored subjects drawn from contemporary life as well as pursuing European plays and forgotten classics. When John Osborne's **Look Back in Anger** was first produced in 1956, and revived in '57, it forced British Theatre into the modern age. At the same time Brecht, Giraudoux, Ionesco and Sartre were also part of the repertoire.

The ambition to discover new work which was challenging, innovative and also of the highest quality became the fulcrum of the Company's course of action. Early Court writers included Arnold Wesker, John Arden, David Storey, Ann Jellicoe, N F Simpson and Edward Bond. They were followed by a generation of writers led by David Hare and Howard Brenton, and in more recent years,

celebrated house writers have included Caryl Churchill, Timberlake Wertenbaker, Robert Holman and Jim Cartwright. Many of their plays are now regarded as modern classics.

In line with the policy of nurturing new writing, the Theatre Upstairs has mainly been seen as a place for exploration and experiment, where writers learn and develop their skills prior to the demands of the Mainstage auditorium. Anne Devlin, Andrea Dunbar, Sarah Daniels, Jim Cartwright, Clare McIntyre, Winsome Pinnnock, and more recently Martin Crimp have, or will in the future, benefit from this process. The Theatre Upstairs proved its value as a focal point for new work with the production of the Chilean writer, Ariel Dorfman's **Death and the Maiden**. More recently, talented young writers as diverse as Jonathan Harvey, Adam Pernak, Phyllis Nagy and Gregory Motton have been shown to great advantage in this space.

David Suchet and Lia Williams in **Oleanna** by David Mamet, 1993

1991, 1992, and 1993 have been record-breaking years at the box-office with capacity houses for productions of **Top Girls**, **Three Birds Alighting on a Field**, **Faith Healer**, **Death and the Maiden** (which moved to The Duke of York's), **Six Degrees of Separation** (which moved to the Comedy Theatre) and most recently **King Lear** and **Oleanna** (which has now moved to The Duke of York's). **Death and the Maiden** and **Six Degrees of Separation** won the Olivier Award for Best Play in 1992 and 1993 respectively. **Three Birds Alighting on a Field** was awarded Best West End Play by the Writer's Guild of Great Britain, and has been successfully revived.

After nearly four decades, the Royal Court Theatre is still a major focus in the country for the production of new work. Scores of plays first seen in Sloane Square are now part of the national and international dramatic repertoire.

Kristin Hewson, Jude Law and Helen Blatch in **Live Like Pigs** by John Arden, 1993

THE ABBEY THEATRE

The Abbey Theatre opened its doors for the first time on December 27th 1904. By merging the literary talents of the Irish Literary Theatre - W B Yeats, Lady Augusta Gregory and Edward Martyn - and the acting experience of the Fay brothers' Irish national Theatre Society, the foundations were laid for the most influential Irish cultural institution in the world.

The Abbey is no less rich in talent now than it was 90 years ago. Alongside its classical repetoire of Synge, O'Casey, Yeats and Lennox Robinson, it continues to feature new plays by such modern masters as Tom Murphy, Hugh Leonard, Frank McGuiness, Billy Roche and Brian Friel while all the time fostering new young writing talent in playwrights like Sebastian Barry, Dermot Bolger, Marina Carr and Jimmy Murphy.

The Abbey acting tradition is renowned and down through the years the theatre has produced such legendary actors as Sarah Algood, Barry Fitzgerald, Ray McAnally, Siobhan McKenna and Cyril Cusack.

The international reputation of the Abbey has never been higher, with the winning of three coveted Tony awards on Broadway in 1992 including Best Play and Best Director for the Abbey production of Brian Friel's **Dancing at Lughnasa**.

The Theatre has also had huge success with its presentations of such international classics as Ibsen's **Hedda Gabler** and Eugene O'Neill's **The Iceman Cometh**.

The Abbey is proud of its historic origins and its record of achievement. But it is a living theatre with its eyes fixed on the opportunities of today and the challenges of tomorrow.

The Abbey Theatre Production of **Dancing at Lughnasa** by Brian Friel

198x125

ALLELUIA!

I tiptoe into the chapel. The choir is up on the organ gallery singing the Alleluia from the Mass that I've just written. It will be recorded and a snatch of it used in the stage play, **The Cavalcaders**. When word gets around that I've arrived the men grow a little uneasy and the choir master rears up on them all. 'Settle down,' he tells them. 'Concentrate.' And so they take another stab at it and when it's over seventy innocent faces seem to peer up over the banister to see what I think of it. Some of them call down to me. Was it alright? How does it sound? I tell them that it was grand. 'One more time,' the choir master says and off they go again, their voices lilting along and the hint of a Wexford accent peeking out through the beautiful curtain of sound that echoes up and down the church.

This is the Wexford Male Voice Choir. As a boy I watched these men going off to work in the factories and the malt stores, watched them hurrying home dirty faced for their dinner. These are the insurance men and the milkmen and the bank clerks and the teachers and the postmen who thronged the bars and the snooker halls and the hurling matches. These are the men who walked the greyhounds and climbed up into the pigeon lofts and conversed in the barber shops of the town way back in those distant days of railway dray horses and half doors. And to think now that they are gathered here in my honour so to speak, to sing my song! Needless to say the notion that I may live forever crosses my mind.

I have rambled up the aisle to stand outside a Confession box. This is the place where as a scrupulous lad I returned time and time again to tell the priest the same little sins over and over. So much so that the man got fed up listening to me and told me that he was going to give me what was called a general absolution which would forgive me for everything I ever did or thought or said and for everything I ever thought I did or said even. And I came out of there walking on air, sailing past the guilty eyed adulterers and drunkards who were waiting in line.

And then there's the marble altar rails. Inside there I served my first mass. The priest on that wintry morning was an elderly man who for some reason or other when he was giving out the Communion insisted that I stand behind him instead of in front which was the proper way. I was raging with him. Half the women from Johns Street had come to see me make my debut as an altar boy. Now I would have to spend the next week or so explaining to them all that I didn't do it wrong, that it was all the priest's fault. My job was to hold the silver plate under the chins of the Communicants just in case the holy Host should take a tumble. We were always led to believe that if this happened the priest would have to come out after mass and get down on his hands and knees and scrub the spot where the host had landed. And guess who would get the blame? The poor boy. Our first customer that morning was a man who had no control over his tongue. It darted in and out of his mouth like a snake on the rampage. In and out and up and down. No logic to it at all. It nearly put the heart crossways in me looking at him. In the end the priest, who could be a fairly contrary sort of a man at the best of times, gave up the ghost altogether and moved along and left him there - Communionless! Out of the corner of my eye I spied the poor man slipping discreetly back to his pew as if everything was hunky dory. The best thing about serving Communion though was that you got the chance to wear the white gloves which I thought were great.

The choir begin to disperse. 'It's a rap,' someone says. So I go to hang on out in the porch as the men come one by one down the winding stairs. I feel like the nervous father of the bride as I wait to shake their hands and thank them for coming and so on. They are wearing their uniforms. No, they didn't wear them especially for the recording. They were singing at a wedding earlier on. Slowly they drift off out into the dwindling daylight to light up their cigarettes and to shoot the breeze for a little while. I mingle with them and soon I come to realise that there are times when small talk can be a beautiful thing. And then they start to scatter off home in all directions -towards The Faythe and Johns Street and Bride Street and Salty Avenue. And as the last few stragglers disappear around the bend I turn to discover that I'm stranded on the far side of a river that I never meant to cross. The choir have carried me here it seems - on a transparent bridge that is now evaporating before my eyes so I may never return again. How did this happen? What's going on? A few minutes ago I was on the other side. All of a sudden I feel like a man! A father! A husband! It's not really fair. I mean this was never supposed to happen to me. I am a child of the sixties. I was never meant to grow any older. NEVER!

The very last member of the choir comes out of the chapel, blessing himself. Was that a smile or a smirk? He knows something. His hair is receding and he is going a little grey at the temples but I know for a fact that I'm older than him. And to make matters worse a child going by calls me mister if you don't mind. Mister though. I'm plagued with the notion that I'm old enough to run for Mayor or something. I'm sure things will never be the same again. Help.

Alle... Alle... Alleluia.

Billy Roche

November 1993

THE *cavalcaders*

by **Billy Roche**

CAST *in order of appearance*

Terry	**Tony Doyle**
Rory	**Barry Barnes**
Josie	**Billy Roche**
Ted	**Gary Lydon**
Breda	**Marie Mullen**
Nuala	**Aisling O'Sullivan**

Director	**Robin Lefèvre**
Designer	**Frank Conway**
Music	**Pat Fitzpatrick**
Lighting Designer	**Trevor Dawson**
Movement	**Geri O'Kelly**
Stage Director	**Colette Morris**
Stage Manager	**Justine Gallaccio**
ASM	**Claire Libby**
Sound	**Dave O'Brien**
Set	**Abbey Theatre Workshop**
Costumes	**Abbey Theatre Wardrobe**
Production Photography	**Charles Collins**
Royal Court Leaflet	**Sightlines**
"Alleluia" sung by the	**Wexford Male Voice Choir**
recorded by	**Dave Nolan**

There will be one interval of 15 minutes

The Abbey Theatre would like to thank the following:

Guinness Ireland; Benson and Hedges; People Newspapers Ltd; Punch Sales Ireland; Belvedere Bags; Mr & Mrs D Barry; Opus II; The Botanic Gardens; Montagus Sandwich Bar. Special thanks to **Joe Kelly** & **Jim Brennan, Dart Heel Bar.**

Wardrobe care by Persil and Comfort courtesy of Lever Brothers Ltd; watches by The Timex Corporation; refrigerators by Electrolux and Philips Major Appliances Ltd.; kettles for rehearsals by Morphy Richards; video for casting purposes by Hitachi; backstage coffee machine by West 9; furniture by Knoll International; freezer for backstage use supplied by Zanussi Ltd 'Now that's a good idea.' Hair by Carole at Edmond's, 19 Beauchamp Place, SW3. Thanks to Casio for use of DAT equipment; closed circuit TV cameras and monitors by Mitsubishi UK Ltd. Natural spring water from Wye Spring Water, 149 Sloane Street, London SW1, tel. 071-730 6977. Overhead projector from W.H. Smith.

BIOGRAPHIES

BILLY ROCHE
(Writer & actor)

Born and lives in Wexford. Began career as singer and musician; formed Roach Band in the late 70's. Plays include: The Wexford Trilogy: A Handful of Stars (Bush Theatre, 1988 - John Whiting Award, Plays & Players Award Best Play, Thames Television Award); Poor Beast in the Rain (Bush Theatre, 1989 - George Devine Award); Belfry (Bush Theatre, 1991 Charrington Fringe Award Best Play, Time Out Theatre Award); Amphibians (RSC, 1992). The Wexford Trilogy also performed at Theatre Royal, Wexford & Abbey Theatre, Dublin. Acting roles include: The Cavalcaders (Abbey, Dublin), A Handful of Stars (Bush), Aristocrats (Hampstead), Poor Beast in the Rain (Abbey, Dublin). TV includes: The Wexford Trilogy (as author), The Bill (as actor). Films include: Strapless by David Hare.

ROBIN LEFEVRE
(Director)

Associate Director Hampstead Theatre.

Productions at Hampstead include: Then and Now, Threads, Writer's Cramp, On the Edge, Fall, Bodies, Spookhouse, Aristocrats (1988 Evening Standard Award, New York Drama Critics Award Best Play), Valued Friends (also Long Wharf, USA).

West End productions include: Outside Edge, Rocket to the Moon, Country Girl, The Big Knife, Are You Lonesome Tonight? (1985 Evening Standard Award Best Musical), The New Revue, The Entertainer.

Other theatre includes: The Wexford Trilogy (Bush Theatre), When We Are Married, On the Ledge (Royal National Theatre), Private Lives (Gate, Dublin), The Curse of the Starving Classes (RSC), Someone Who'll Watch Over Me (Hampstead, Vaudeville, Abbey, Broadway).

FRANK CONWAY
(Designer)

Head of Design at the Abbey Theatre & Resident Designer at Druid Theatre Co.

Theatre design includes work for Royal Court, Greenwich Theatre, Shakespeare in the Park (New York), Shakespeare Festival (Ontario), all leading Irish companies.

TV and film design includes: The Woman Who Married Clark Gable, Da, The Field, The Juliet Letters. Lectures on design extensively.

PAT FITZPATRICK
(Music)

Theatre work includes: Pirates of Penzance, The Rocky Horror Show (SFX), The Raven Beckons (Riverbank), Private Lives, The Cherry Orchard (Gate, Dublin), Silverlands (Abbey, Dublin). Extensive TV work; currently music director for Rebecca Storm.

TREVOR DAWSON
(Lighting Designer)

Theatre lighting designs include: Equus, The Seagull, A Midsummer Night's Dream, Mary Stuart, The Mikado, Northern Star and many others (Lyric, Belfast); How the Other Half Loves (Olympia, Dublin); A Christmas Carol, A Woman of No Importance, Arrah-Na-Pogue, The Recruiting Officer, Uncle Vanya, The Importance of Being Earnest, The Rivals, Absurd Person Singular, Salome (Gate, Dublin); The Silver Dollar Boys, You Can't Take it With You, The Silver Tassie, Dancing at Lughnasa, Faith Healer, The Plough and the Stars, Conversations on a Homecoming, Moving, Purple Dust, The Cuchulainn Cycle, Masks of Transformation, Sacred Mysteries & Strange Occurence on Ireland's Eye, A Crucial Week in the Life of a Grocer's Assistant, The Trojan Women (Abbey, Dublin).

GERI O'KELLY
(Movement)

Worked as dancer & choreographer.

Theatre choreography includes: The Merchant of Venice, The Drums of Father Ned, Ring Round the Moon, A Child's Christmas in Wales, You Can't Take It With You, Dark Lady, Purple Dust; Danny, The Witch and The Gobbin (Abbey, Dublin); The Adventures of Mr. Toad, The Sound of Music, The Wizard of Oz, Snoopy the Musical (Olympia, Dublin); The Rocky Horror Show (SFX); Carousel (Tivoli); Romeo & Juliet, The London Vertigo, Private Lives, The Cherry Orchard, A Midsummer Night's Dream (Gate, Dublin).

As actor/dancer work includes: Gypsy, The Cuchulainn Cycle (Gaiety, Dublin).

TONY DOYLE

Theatre includes: The Gigli Concert (Abbey, Almeida); Too Late for Logic (Abbey); Mr. Joyce is Leaving Paris, The Birthday Party, Da, John Bull's Other Island, The Plough and the Stars, Translations.

TV includes: Lovers of the Lake, Macbeth, The Contractor, The Hen House, Arise and Go Now, Treaty, Children of the North, Murder in Eden, Between the Lines.

Film includes: Loophole, Who Dares Wins, Eat the Peach, Devil's Paradise, Secret Friends, Damage.

BARRY BARNES

Theatre includes: The Caretaker (Focus); Twelfth Night (Gate, Dublin); Antigone, Shadow and Substance (Druid Theatre Co); Love and a Bottle, A Handful of Stars (Rough Magic); John Bull's Other Island, Borstal Boy, The Plough and the Stars, The Scatterin' (Gaiety, Dublin); The Lament for Arthur Cleary (7:84 Theatre Co); The Silver Tassie, You Can't Take it With You (Abbey, Dublin).

TV & film includes: Joy Street, Fair City.

GARY LYDON

Theatre includes: A Handful of Stars, Poor Beast in the Rain (Best Actor Award for Georgie), Belfry (Bush Theatre, Theatre Royal, Wexford, Abbey, Dublin); Grace in America (Old Red Lion); Same Old Moon (Nuffield, Southampton); Battle of the Aughrim, BAC, Normal Heart, Young Europeans (Project Arts Centre); What the Butler Saw, Fool for Love, Equus, Fire Raisers, Trumpets and Raspberries (Riff Raff Theatre, Wexford); Conversations on a Homecoming (Abbey, Dublin).

TV & film includes: Hard Cases, The Bill, Bergerac, Strapless, The Wexford Trilogy.

Radio includes: Boor Beast in the Rain, Pioneers in Ingolstadt.

MARIE MULLEN

Founder member of Druid Theatre Co.

Theatre for Druid includes: The Playboy of the Western World, Bailegangaire, A Doll's House, The Glass Menagerie.

Other theatre includes: King Lear, The Man of Mode (RSC); The Plough and the Stars, The Power of Darkness, Conversations on a Homecoming, Drama at Inish, A Crucial Week in the Life of a Grocer's Assistant (Abbey, Dublin).

AISLING O'SULLIVAN

Theatre includes: The Quirke Estate (Project Arts Centre); The Murphy Initiative, The Power of Darkness, The Corsican Brothers, Away Alone, The Winter Thief, The Countess Cathleen, Silverlands, The Honey Spike (Abbey, Dublin).

The Almeida Theatre Company

presents

3 February - 31 March

The Life of Galileo

Brecht's masterpiece

In a new version
by **David Hare**
with **Richard Griffiths**

WORLD PREMIERE

7 - 10 April

Butterfly Kiss

An acerbic comedy.
Lily Ross has
murdered her mother...
by **Phyllis Nagy**

For further information and tickets
call the Box Office on

071 359 4404

ALMEIDA STREET LONDON N1 1TA
Registered Charity

HOW THE ROYAL COURT IS BROUGHT TO YOU...

*The English Stage Company at the Royal Court Theatre is supported financially by a wide range of public bodies and private companies, as well as its own trading activities. The theatre receives its principal funding from the **Arts Council of Great Britain**, which has supported the Royal Court since 1956. The **Royal Borough of Kensington & Chelsea** gives an annual grant to the Royal Court Young People's Theatre and provides some of its staff. The **London Boroughs Grants Committee** contributes to the cost of productions in the Theatre Upstairs.*

*Other parts of the Royal Court's activities are made possible by business sponsorships. Several of these sponsors have made a long term commitment. 1994 will see the fourth Barclays New Stages Festival of new theatre, which has been supported throughout by **Barclays Bank**. **British Gas North Thames** has so far supported three years of the Royal Court's Education Programme. Now in its 26th year, the Young Writers' Festival has been sponsored by **Marks and Spencer** since 1991. The latest sponsorship by **WH Smith** has been to help make the launch of the new Friends of the Royal Court scheme so successful.*

*In 1988 the Royal Court launched the **Olivier Building Appeal** to raise funds to restore, repair and improve the theatre building. So far nearly £700,000 has been raised. The theatre has new bars and front of house areas, new roofs, air conditioning and central heating boilers and a rehearsal room and work will start in the new year to restore and clean the theatre's facade. This would not have been possible without a very large number of generous supporters and the significant contributions from the **Theatres' Restoration Fund**, the **Rayne Foundation**, the **Foundation for Sport and the Arts** and the **Arts Council's Incentive Funding Scheme**.*

*The **Gerald Chapman Award** was founded in 1988 to train and develop young theatre directors. It is now jointly funded by the Royal Court and **BBC Television**. The **ITV Companies** fund the **Regional Theatre Young Directors Scheme**, with which the Royal Court has been associated for many years.*

*1993 has seen the start of a new association with the **Audrey Skirball-Kenis Theatre** of Los Angeles. The Skirball Foundation is funding a Playwrights Programme at the Royal Court. Exchange visits for writers between Britain and the USA complement the greatly increased programme of reading and workshops which have fortified the Royal Court's capability to develop new plays.*

*The Royal Court earns the rest of money it needs to operate from the Box Office, from other trading and from the transfers of plays such as **Death and the Maiden**, **Six Degrees of Separation** and currently **Oleanna** to the West End. But without public subsidy it would close immediately and its unique place in British Theatre would be lost. The Arts Council faces the threat of a £5 million cut in its grant from the government next year. This would certainly mean large cuts in the Arts Council grants to theatres. If you care about the future of arts in this country, please write to your MP and say so.*

Coming Next

TICKETS
FROM ONLY
£5

MAIN HOUSE

from 16 February
The Royal Court Theatre presents

The Kitchen

**by Arnold Wesker
Directed by Stephen Daldry**

March/April
*The Royal Court Theatre &
The Wrestling School present*

Hated Nightfall

**written & directed by
Howard Barker**

PLATFORM
PERFORMANCES

supported by Random House/
Waterstone's Booksellers

17 January at 6.15pm

Naomi Wolf

2 February at 6.15pm

Jonathan Mendes
& Will Self

in conversation

THEATRE UPSTAIRS

12 - 29 January
The Royal Court Theatre presents

Penetrator

**written & directed by
Anthony Neilson**

February/March
*The Royal Court Theatre in
association with the Royal
National Theatre Studio present*

The Madness of
Esme and Shaz

**by Sarah Daniels
directed by Jessica Dromgoole**

March
*The Royal Court Young People's
Theatre presents*

Pocahontas WORKING TITLE

**written by Steve Shill
music by Stephen Warbeck
directed by Roxana Silbert**

April
The Royal Court Theatre presents

My Night with Reg

by Kevin Elyot

DUKE OF YORK'S THEATRE

The Royal Court Theatre production

Oleanna

written by David Mamet   directed by Harold Pinter

RSC

**ROYAL
SHAKESPEARE
COMPANY**

WORLD PREMIERE

Unfinished Business

by Michael Hastings

As Britain nervously awaits news of Hitler's plan to invade, not everyone is hoping he will fail. Deep in the heart of England's Shires, a group of fascist aristocrats wait nervously to hear news, any news. Meanwhile, the young son of the house is conducting a passionate affair with a maid in the attic above their heads...

Fifty years later an old man waits patiently in a retirement home. Unexpected visitors bring the past closer than he could ever have imagined.

Unfinished lives...
unfinished business...

This new play, from the author of *Tom and Viv*, *Gloo Joo* and *A Dream of People*, crosses and re-crosses time to create a dark, funny and poignant world.

**Previews from 12 January
Opens 19 January in The Pit**

**Barbican Box Office
071 638 8891**

Council Funded

THE OLIVIER BUILDING APPEAL

The Royal Court reached the ripe old age of 100 in September 1988. The theatre was showing its age somewhat, and the centenary was celebrated by the launch of the Olivier Appeal, for £800,000 to repair and improve the building.

*Laurence Olivier's long association with the Court began as a schoolboy. He was given "a splendid seat in the Dress Circle" to see his first Shakespeare, **Henry IV Part 2** and was later to appear as Malcolm in **Macbeth** (in modern dress) in a Barry Jackson production, visiting from the Birmingham Repertory Theatre in 1928. His line of parts also included the Lord in the Prologue of **The Taming of the Shrew**. This early connection and his astonishing return in **The Entertainer**, which changed the direction of his career in 1957, made it natural that he should be the Appeal Patron. After his death, Joan Plowright CBE, the Lady Olivier, consented to take over as Patron.*

We are now three-quarters of the way to our target. With the generous gifts of our many friends and donors, and an award from the Arts Council's Incentive Fund, we have enlarged and redecorated the bars and front of house areas, installed a new central heating boiler and new air conditioning equipment in both theatres, rewired many parts of the building, redecorated the dressing rooms and we are gradually upgrading the lighting and sound equipment.

With the help of the Theatre Restoration Fund, work has now been completed on building a rehearsal room and replacing the ancient roofs. The Foundation for Sport and the Arts have promised a grant which will enable us to restore the faded Victorian facade of the theatre. So, much is being done, but much remains to do, to improve the technical facilities backstage which will open up new possibilities for our set designers.

*Can you help? A tour of the theatre, including its more picturesque parts, can be arranged by ringing Becky Shaw on **071 730 5174**. If you would like to help with an event or a gift please ring Graham Cowley, General Manager, on the same number.*

Laurence Olivier 1907-1989
Photo: Snowdon

'Secure the Theatre's future, and take it forward towards the new century. For the health of the whole theatrical life of Britain it is essential that this greatly all-providing theatre we love so much and wish so well continues to prosper.'
Laurence Olivier (1988)

THE CAVALCADERS

Cast

Terry
Josie
Rory
Ted
Breda
Nuala

The play is set in a small town in Ireland. It opens in the present day, flashing back to about seven years ago.

Stage Setting

The main stage setting is an old fashioned shoemaker's shop with a small stocky counter. The shop is cluttered with mended shoes which are stacked on shelves behind the counter and there is a heap of mended and broken uncollected shoes piled up all around from the floor to the ceiling. There are two doors – one leading to the street, the other to a back room and toilet. There is a bench, and tucked away in a corner there is an old battered piano which is usually covered up with a sheet. There is one window, situated behind the counter.

ACT ONE

Lights rise on the shop. TERRY *is standing in the half light which filters in from the street. It is night.* TERRY, *who does not look too well, is dressed in a heavy overcoat and his overall appearance suggests that life has taken its toll on him*

RORY (*off*). I think this auld fuse is gone, Terry.

TERRY. What's that?

RORY (*entering*). I say I think this auld fuse is gone.

TERRY. There's probably one in that auld drawers there I'd say.

RORY. Yeh reckon? . . . Wait 'til I have a gike . . . Your man thinks he should be in and out of here in about a fortnight yeh know.

TERRY. Who's that?

RORY. Whatshisname – the lad who's doin' the job for me. Oh by the way, while I think of it, if you're wantin' any souvenirs out of this place now, you'd better speak up because it'll all be gone out of here by this time tomorrow. So speak now or forever hold your peace as the fella says. Whist! . . . I'll try this one . . . This place is goin' to be run properly. In and out. None of this hangin' on to stuff for years on end at all. If they're not back to collect the article in question within a month it'll be sold off or given a way to charity. (*He goes off.*) . . . Sure there's a shoe in there and it must be there this five years if not more . . . More I'd say!

The light comes on.

How's that?

TERRY. That's her.

RORY. Is that it, yeah?

TERRY. Yeah . . . It's very weak, mind yeh. I'd say that auld bulb is goin'.

RORY (*entering*). Huh?

TERRY. I say that auld bulb is nearly bet.

RORY. Yeah? (*He picks up a dusty shoe.*) There it is there Terry, look. That must be there this five or six years. That used to belong to that one legged man from The Faythe, yeh know. Whatshisname – he was an insurance man. Kelly! He was in the bed alongside Josie in the hospital that time. The poor divil lost his other leg after – the week before he died. 'There he is now,' says Josie, 'without a leg to stand on.' (*He chuckles sadly.*) Poor auld Josie hah! . . . Wait 'til yeh see what I'm goin' to do with this place though Terry. A new counter along here. And bare floorboards all the way out to the door – yeh know all varnished and all. And there'll be a bench here for people to sit on while they're waitin'.

TERRY. Waitin' for what?

RORY. Their shoes! In and out mate. There's none of this, 'call back in three weeks' time,' now yeh know. Those days are gone, boy!

TERRY. A Chinese takeaway be Jaysus!

RORY. The shelves'll be all along here. And against the back wall there'll be all the machinery and all. Yeh should see the gadgets we're gettin' though Terry, I'm not coddin' yeh boy . . . Yeh know I can teach a man now in about three weeks what it used to take a year to perfect in the auld days. That's a fact boy!

TERRY. Yeah but it can't be the same job though can it?

RORY. It is. Better!

TERRY. It couldn't be! I mean where's the skill? Where's the attention to detail?

RORY. Attention to detail! Are yeh coddin' me or what? I mean do you seriously think now that meself and Ted and Josie paid any attention to detail? Hah? (*He shakes his head and chuckles.*)

TERRY. I suppose! . . . How's the little one?

RORY. Alright. She's makin' her Communion next month.

TERRY. Is she? Jaysus hah!

RORY. Oh she's a real little madam now the same one! . . . I was lyin' in the bed the other mornin' there though Terry yeh know and next I hears her stirrin' inside the other room. She gets out and toddles across the landin' to the bathroom – a little sleepy head on her. I hear her do a little widdle then flush the toilet after her and then she goes runnin' back to her little warm bed again and I think to meself, 'How did I get her this far at all eh?' Yeh know! . . . They're deadly little sounds though . . . (*He chuckles and basks in the thought of it all.*) . . . I'll go over and get a bulb for that I think because . . . Tell the truth now Terry, I bet you'll be just as glad to see the back of this auld place won't yeh? Hah?

TERRY. Ah I don't know. I mean to say I had me moments here like yeh know.

RORY. Yeah but they were far and few between though Terry weren't they? Hah? admit it now. I tell yeh, yeh already look like a bit of a stranger to the place as it is.

TERRY. Do I?

RORY. Yeah . . . I won't be a minute. Will you be alright there?

TERRY. Yeah.

RORY leaves. Pause. TERRY gazes around him and suddenly an icy shiver seems to creep over him and he whips his head towards the doorway of the back room. He gasps. Pause. He turns to look up at the squinting bulb.

TERRY. Mmn . . .

The bulb dies. Darkness. Lights rise on the shop. JOSIE is standing in the middle of the shop with a toilet roll in his hand, singing at the top of his voice. RORY and TED are up at the window.

JOSIE(*singing*). Oh sole mio
My arse is sore
Oh please don't ask me
To go no more . . .

TED. Look at her. Out of this world ain't she?

RORY. Yeah. Deadly even legs hasn't she? Look, every fella on the street is gawkin 'at her. Look at the state of your man Poe the undertaker lookin' at her. He's nearly after jawlockin' himself there .

JOSIE (*singing*). Have mercy
Oh can 't you see . . .

TED. I 'd give a week's wages boy just to wake up beside her one mornin', do yeh know that .

RORY. That' s nice of yeh.

TED. No I would though – a week's wages I'd give boy!

JOSIE (*sings*). That we surrender
My arse and me.

JOSIE exits to the back room.

RORY. She is somethin' else though ain't she? Hah? Beautiful Bundoran hah!

TERRY enters, younger and more robust than before.

TERRY. Lord Jaysus ain't that awful – every time I turn me back.

The pair of you must think it's a whorehouse I'm runnin' here or somethin', do yeh. Hah? Come down out of there and get back to work out of that.

RORY (*climbing down*). She's deadly boy, I don't care what anyone says.

TERRY. Yes, a whorehouse you must think you're in or somethin'. Who is it, my little bank girl?

RORY. Yeah. Deadly she is boy! I don't care.

TERRY (*climbing up beside* TED). Give us a look at her. She's late today – she must have had a bit of trouble with her balance sheet . . . Oh be the Lort! I'm in love.

TED. What do yeh think of her?

TERRY. What do I think of her? I think she's just . . . What's the word I'm searchin' for?

RORY. Beautiful.

TERRY. Class . . . Do yeh know what I feel now when I look at her?

TED. Yeah – horny.

TERRY. I feel a warm glow inside of me.

RORY. And I second that emotion. I'd marry her in the mornin' boy if she's have me.

TERRY. Now there's a man who appreciates the finer things in life. Not like you. You're only wantin' to jump on the girl's bones.

TED. That's true. He's right there.

RORY (*sings*). Beautiful Bundoran . . .

TERRY. Did yeh notice that lads, the farther away she gets, the nicer she looks. (To RORY.) I'm goin' to tell your wife on you boy!

RORY. Did yeh see the state of your man Poe lookin' at her?

TERRY. Yeah, he's after catchin' his big chin in the spokes of his bike, look. Funerals'll never be the same again.

RORY. He's probably measurin' her from afar.

BREDA *enters*.

TERRY. Look at the dirt of that window lads.

TED. Yeah, the state of it! (*They both polish and rub.*)

BREDA. I'm not surprised with the pair of you foggin' it up.

RORY (*sings*). Beautiful Bundoran.

TERRY (*climbing down*). Are yeh alright hon?

BREDA. Yeh needn't bother tryin' to plomás me at all boy.

TERRY. Why, what's wrong with yeh?

BREDA. Where's me shoe?

TERRY. What?

BREDA. Me shoe, me shoe. Where is it?

TERRY. Did they not bring that over to you?

BREDA. Well if they did I wouldn't be here lookin' for it now would I? I wouldn't mind but I was goin' to a dinner dance last night and everything. There I was heckin' around me bedroom like a schoolgirl – one shoe on me. I had to get a loan of a pair in the end.

TERRY. I don't know . . . (*He finds the shoe.*)

Did I not tell you to bring that over to Breda when it was mended?

RORY. No, yeh did not.

TED. Yeh needn't bother lookin' at me either.

TERRY. Well I told one of yez. It must have been the other fella I told. It was, too. Hang on Breda.

TERRY goes *off into the back room and we hear him shouting at* JOSIE.

Did I not tell you to bring that shoe over to Breda when it was mended. I wouldn't mind but the woman was waitin' on it too to go to a reunion. She said she was heckin' around the place like a schoolgirl with one shoe on her, lookin' for this. I'm not coddin' yeh if I don't do everythin' meself around here it just don't get done. Well there's goin' to be big changes around here from now on I can tell yeh. Yes, big changes there's goin' to be!

TERRY *returns with the shoe.*

Here y'are Breda – on the house hon.

BREDA. I should think so too. Yeh needn't bother wrappin' it. I'm goin' to wear it. I've a shoe and a slipper on me at the moment. I'm like an orphan of the storm here, so I am.

She sits on the bench to put her shoe on. TERRY *comes out to her.*

TERRY. Yeh could do with a bit of a stitch in that other shoe too Breda I don't mind tellin' yeh.

BREDA. It's alright, I'll get out of here while I'm ahead.

TERRY. No, we'll put a stitch in that for yeh while you're here. Can't have you goin' around the place slipshod now can we? Hah? (*He bends to slip off her shoe.*) Here y'are Ted, put a stitch in that for Breda there will yeh. Do yeh see that stack of shoes there Breda? Take a pair of them for yourself if yeh want – do yeh for knockin' around in.

BREDA. Yeah and end up with someone else's bunions, no thanks.

TERRY (*caressing her feet*). I know a good cure for bunions.

BREDA. I bet yeh do and all.

TERRY. I do though . . . Did anyone ever tell yeh that yeh had lovely little dainty feet?

BREDA. Yeah, someone did mention that to me one time alright.

TERRY. Well he knew what he was talkin' about whoever he was.

RORY. He's real plomásey Breda ain't he? Hah?

BREDA. Shut up you and leave him alone. Go ahead, what were yeh sayin'?

TERRY. What?

RORY. Breda's enjoyin' it.

TERRY. I love women with dainty feet yeh know. It's the first thing I look for.

BREDA. Is it?

TERRY. Mmn . . .

RORY. I love women wheelin' prams. And I love watchin' women drivin'. I love women on bicycles too. And women wearin' glasses. And I like . . .

TED. Yeah alright, we get the message.

RORY *laughs.* TERRY *and* BREDA *are looking into each other's eyes,* BREDA *is flirting with him with her toes.*

TERRY. Did yeh meet anyone interestin' last night?

BREDA. No.

RORY. What band was playin' at it Breda?

BREDA. The Salinger Brothers.

TERRY. The only three of their kind in captivity hah!

RORY. Yeah. 'She Taught Me to Yodel.'

TED. It's a pity someone wouldn't teach them to sing.

RORY. Did yeh ever notice lads, a great collective sigh goes up every time they play the National Anthem.

TERRY. Hey, don't mock the afflicted boy! . . . So who did yeh dance with all night then?

BREDA. Anyone who asked me.

TERRY. Hah? Jaysus that's not like you, Breda. You used to be very particular.

BREDA. Yeah. That was before the flood though.

TERRY chuckles.

TED. Here y'are Breda, try that on for size.

TERRY. Give it here. (TERRY *takes the shoe and slips it on her foot.*)

TED. You're like Cinderella there Breda.

BREDA. Yeah – after the ball was over!

TERRY. Now . . . How's that.

BREDA (*stands up and wriggles her toes*). Grand . . . I don't owe yeh anythin' then?

TERRY No – not a cent!

BREDA That's good . . . I must come in here more often.

BREDA gives a little wave and heads for the door.

TERRY I'll see yeh hon.

RORY. Bye Breda.

BREDA leaves. JOSIE enters.

TED. See yeh Breda.

JOSIE. What was that all about?

RORY. Someone forgot to bring Breda's shoe over to her and she was waitin' on it to go to a reunion last night.

JOSIE. Yeah and the auld gom gets the feckin' blame for it here of course . . . (*He puts on his jacket.*) . . . I'm off. Give us me money will yeh. A fiver. (TERRY *throws him a dirty look.*) . . . Two pairs of black there and that brown one behind yeh.

TERRY. Yeah?

JOSIE. And the sandal for whathisname – Friar Tuck.

TERRY. Oh yeah .

JOSIE. He hates payin' money out boy.

TERRY (*wrapping a pair of shoes up in newspaper*). Well listen here, do yeh know what you'll do for me, drop these in to Mrs Kinsella on your way home will yeh. She owes me a fiver. You can keep that then.

JOSIE. I'm not goin' home yet. I'm wantin' to get a couple of large bottles before I go home so . . . I'll tell yeh what I'll do, you give me a sub of three quid and I'll drop these up to her on me way home after . . .

TERRY. It's alright. Here, give them back to me. Here's your fiver. Go ahead.

JOSIE. What? (*He chuckles.*) Are yeh headin' over for one Ted?

TED. Yeah, just a sec . . . (*He puts his tools away.*) Are yeh goin' for a pint Rory?

RORY. No, I'm goin' straight home.

JOSIE. Oh the apron strings boy! The apron strings! Hurry up Ted, will yeh.

TERRY. You fella don't forget we've a practice tonight.

RORY. What time?

TERRY. Seven sharp.

JOSIE. Well make sure it is sharp then.

RORY. Why, have yeh a heavy date on or somethin' Josie?

JOSIE. Yeah, a rendezous with a couple of large bottles. Come on Ted will yeh for Jaysus sake, you're like an auld woman there . . .

RORY. What are we doin' tonight anyway Terry? Anything adventurous in mind?

TERRY. No.

JOSIE. Where do you think yeh are eh boy – in the French Foreign Legion or somethin'? . . . Adventurous! Are yeh right?

TED. Yeah . . .

NUALA *enters as* TED *and* JOSIE *are leaving.*

I hope you have dainty feet, have yeh?

NUALA. What?

JOSIE. She has dainty hands anyway, I can tell yeh.

TED. How do you know?

JOSIE. Because I bought two oranges off of her this mornin' and they were like a couple of melons in her hands and goosegobs in mine, when I took them out of the bag.

TED. Show us. (*He takes her hand.*) They are too! You'll be devoured.

NUALA. What?

TED *bends to kiss her hand.* NUALA *is flattered by it all.*

RORY. Hey Nuala, do you ever get any of the bank clerks comin' into the shop?

NUALA. Yeah, sometimes. Why?

RORY. No reason. Just wonderin'.

JOSIE. Look at Jacques LePouvier, where he is. (*To* TED.) Come on. (*They leave.*)

NUALA. Would yeh have five pounds in small change to spare, Terry?

TERRY. Yeah, no problem . . . You go ahead home, Rory, leave that. Yeh have to be back down by seven, don't forget.

RORY. Yeah right . . . (*He gets his coat.*) . . . Is the shop shut over there or what, Nuala?

NUALA. Yeah, I shut up for about an hour or so. Why, are yeh wantin' somethin'?

RORY. No it's alright. I'll get it in Breens on my way up. I'm just wantin' to get the young one a bar of chocolate or somethin' that's all . . . There's some change down in the bottom drawer there I think, Terry.

TERRY. What? Is there? Oh , right . . .

RORY. Well Nuala, have yeh settled in yet, yeah?

NUALA. Settled in?

RORY. Yeah. To town life, I mean?

NUALA. Oh yeah. More or less.

RORY. That's good. You've got used to our wily ways, hah?

NUALA *smiles and nods. She stares at* RORY *in a vacant sort of way.* RORY *feels a little uneasy beneath her strange gaze.*

Did yeh get it Terry?

TERRY. Yeah. Go ahead.

RORY. Right. I'll see yeh tonight then Terry, eh?

TERRY. Right. Try and get here on time, will yeh. Stop the other fella whingin'.

RORY (*leaving*). OK. See yeh, Nuala.

NUALA. Bye.

Silence. TERRY looks into NUALA's eyes . Pause. Slowly NUALA goes across and locks the door. She pulls down the blind on it too. TERRY pulls down the blind on the window. They turn to look at each other. Then NUALA begins to walk slowly towards him, coming in behind the counter, rushing into his arms. They kiss and slither to the floor. Lights down. Lights rise. TERRY is standing in the half light, the heavy overcoat on him. There is a loud rapping on the door. He goes across and opens it. TED and JOSIE enter.

JOSIE (*switching on the light*). What are yeh doin 'in the dark, eh boy – playin' with yourself or somethin'?

TERRY. What? I 'm only after gettin' here meself. I have the kettle on .

TED. Any sign of the other fella yet?

TERRY. No.

TED. He must be doin' the ironin'.

JOSIE. Well it's seven now. I'm goin' at half eight on the dot. An hour and a half, yeh said.

TERRY. Yeah, yeah, yeah. What are yeh wantin'? Tea or coffee?

TED. I'll have a tea.

TERRY. Josie?

JOSIE. None of them.

TERRY is behind the counter making the tea.

TED. Jaysus, she really has Rory by the short and curlies though lads, hasn't she? Hah? He can't stir boy.

JOSIE. Leave the girl alone. She's alright.

TED. Do yeh hear Josie, all of a sudden . . . You'd think he was a rock of sense there or somethin'.

JOSIE sniggers. TED goes and whips the sheet from the piano. He tinkles.

JOSIE. Have we any shillin's worth talkin' about in the kitty Terry?

TERRY. Yeah, we have a few bob behind us alright, why?

JOSIE. Just wonderin' . . . I don t suppose there's any chance of a . . .

TERRY. No – no chance! . . . We have expenses. Travellin' expenses, cleanin', sheet music . . .

JOSIE. Yeah alright I get the picture. Just askin'.

TED. Ask, for you shall receive hah!

JOSIE. Yeah. How wrong can yeh be! . . .

TED. Did yeh get home at all Terry, no?

TERRY. No.

TED. And did yeh get anything to eat?

TERRY. Yeah I slipped across for a sandwich.

TED. Yeah? . . . There's dedication, boy! I think this auld thing is after slippin' again Terry.

TERRY. Is it?

TED. Yeah. Yeh might get us out your uncle Eamon's auld tunin' fork there, will yeh. Here he is now. It's about time too.

RORY (*entering*). What? But sure it's only gone seven.

TED. Oh yeah!

RORY. What?

TERRY. Rory, what are you wantin' – tea or coffee?

RORY. Coffee.

TERRY. Of course you'd have to be awkward.

RORY. What?

TED. Yeah, awkward arse.

RORY. What's awkward about it?

TERRY. Here . . . Jacques LePouvier! Now, first things first. Where's the suits?

RORY. They're up in my house.

TERRY. Well, take them down to the cleaners tomorrow will yeh? Right?

RORY. Yeah.

TERRY. Don't forget now.

JOSIE. That reminds me, there's an auld button missin' off my jacket too. I must eh . . .

TED. Rory's missus'll sew that back on for yeh, Josie.

RORY. You'll be lucky.

TED. Tell her I'll be up to start those presses for her tomorrow evenin'.

RORY. Yeah, where did I hear that before?

TED. No, I will though . Straight up!

TERRY. The suits'll be left in here after they're cleaned. Everybody come down here to change into them because there's no proper dressin' rooms or anythin' up above. And afterwards come back here again and change back into your own clothes. Do not go into the bar wearin' the suit.It gives a wrong impression.

RORY. Yeah Josie – makin' a holy show of us.

JOSIE. Can we get on with it now?

TED. Yeah come on, let's get on it.

RORY. Yeah, some of us have homes to go to yeh know.

JOSIE. We know!

RORY. Who is this Jacques LePouviarse anyway?

JOSIE. LePouvier.

TERRY. What? Here y'are Ted. (*The tuning fork.*)

JOSIE. He was a French chap who used to come home to Breens every summer. We all thought we were a right crowd of hard chaws until he arrived. We had a couple of pairs of boxin' gloves, yeh know, and we used to be sparrin' one another out on the street and all. Meself and Terry and little Dinky Doyle and all. Well, your man came over boy and he knocked seven kinds of shite out of the whole lot of us, Terry, didn't he?

TERRY. Yeah.

TED. That's nearly a half tone down, Terry. No wonder hah!

TERRY. Mmn . . .

JOSIE. He was as fast. And hard! You'd think your head was goin' to come off your shoulders when he'd hit yeh, that's all . . . Do yeh remember the day he knocked out poor auld Poe Terry? Dead as a cock, boy! Your man Poe got all serious, yeh know, and the next thing Jacques hauls off and hits him a box in the jaw, knocks him as dead as a cock. I'm not coddin' yeh he looked like a corpse in the gutter. Dinky crossed his arms over his chest and sent a message up to his Da to come down and bury him. The laughs of Jacques at that! He was a gas man though, Terry, wasn't he? Hah? Bon Jour your whore tonight for sure hah! All the girls used to be after him, boy – Breda and all.

RORY. Yeah?

JOSIE. Oh yeah. He was a good lookin' fella like, yeh know. Do yeh remember Dinky, Terry? (*He imitates Dinky's boxing stance.*)

TERRY. Yeah . . . I tried to get Rogan to take on Jacques one time. Rogan would've knackered him alright I'd say.

JOSIE. I don't know.

TERRY. Ah but sure Rogan was like chain lightnin' himself, Josie. And hard too! He gave the Bullet O'Brien a run for his money one night, yeh know. And the Bullet was a handy boxer.

JOSIE. Yeah?

TERRY. Oh yeah. Up the back of the C.Y. The blood was pumpin' out of the pair of them I believe.

JOSIE *thinks about it and shrugs.*

RORY. But sure I heard your man Rogan was a fair man for the women himself was he?

JOSIE *throws him a dirty look. An awkward silence.*

JOSIE Poor auld Jacques though hah! . . . He broke one of my teeth too, the bastard! . . .

TERRY *is putting the tuning fork back in its proper place behind the counter.* TED *is playing the scale, singing in harmony to it.* RORY *clears his throat and paces. The others begin to warm up also.* RORY *joins in with* TED, *singing the bass line.* JOSIE *sings 'Carrig River'.* TERRY *comes to join the others around the piano. He coughs and clears his throat etc.*

RORY (*chanting*). Dominic have the biscuits come . . . Dominic have the biscuits come.

JOSIE (*sings*). 'Tis well I do remember when together we did roam. Through the lonely dells of Carrig where the woodcock makes his home. All nature it is smiling upon each rocky side.

TED. Are yez right?

TERRY. Yeah, go ahead.

TED. Rory?

RORY. Yeah.

TED. What?

RORY. No, hang on though . . . (*He goes to fetch his coffee.*) Right.

TERRY *gives* TED *the bend and they launch into a barber shop version of 'I'm Leaning on the Lampost on the Corner of the Street'.*

SONG. I 'm Leaning On The Lamppost On The Corner Of The
  Street
Until A Certain Little Lady Comes By .
Oh Me, Oh My, I Hope That Little Lady Comes By.
She's Absolutely Marvellous And Absolutely Wonderful
That Anyone Can Understand Why
I'm Leaning On The Lampost On The Corner Of The Street
Until A Certain Little Lady Comes By.

This verse is repeated softly as TERRY *speaks over it.*

TERRY. Hello Ladies And Gentlemen. You're listening to The
  Cavalcaders . For the next hour or so we will be bringing you a
  selection of barber shop songs along with some beautiful
  classic love songs from the world of popular music. I do hope
  you enjoy the show.

SONG. I'm Leaning On the Lampost At The Corner Of The
  Street
Until A Certain Little Lady Comes By . . .

The song ends. BREDA *enters, carrying a carrier bag which contains a plate of sandwiches and a plate of cakes and a clean tea-towel-come-table-cloth.*

BREDA. Jaysus, is that the time already.

TERRY. What?

RORY. Nice one Breda.

JOSIE. Yeah – very droll Breda.

TED. Make mine with a little cucumber on the side, Breda will
  yeh.

BREDA. You'll be lucky.

TERRY. Are yeh alright Breda?

BREDA (*going behind the counter*). Yeah.

RORY. Do you always finish like that Ted?

TED. Like what?

RORY. That abrupt like?

TED. I always play it like that. Why?

RORY. No it just sounded a bit whatdoyoucallit like, yeh know.

TERRY *smiles fondly at* BREDA *as she goes calmly about her work.*

TED. What? (TED *demonstrates*. RORY *nods dubiously*.)

JOSIE (*making a face at* RORY *and then to* TED).Come on.

TED (*to* TERRY). One Heart?

TERRY. Yeah.

TED *plays the introduction . They sing.*

One heart broken
One star falling from the sky
One word spoken
My baby's telling me goodbye.

One day, some day
My dreams will all come true you'll see and then
One day, some day
My baby's coming home to me again.

The voices go lilting over one another at this point. NUALA appears in the doorway to bask in the sound of The Cavalcaders. BREDA has finished her work setting out the plates on the table cloth on the counter, washing the mugs and making a fresh pot of tea etc.

NUALA. Beautiful isn't it?

BREDA. Mmn.

NUALA. I love that song . . . And everyone just walks on by . . .

BREDA. Yeah! Jaysus in the auld days this whole neighbourhood 'd be hoppin' whenever the boys were rehearsin' here.

NUALA. Yeah?

BREDA Oh yeah. The Cavalcaders! Terry's uncle Eamon was the boss that time. Terry and Josie were only the garsúns of the group . . . (*She chuckles.*) . . . The pair of them had an awful job convincin' Eamon to let them do a few new numbers. They did, 'Rag Doll,' and , 'Monday, Monday.' They used to do a right job on 'Monday, Monday.' . . . The whole street used to be out listenin' to them though, yeh know – women sittin' on window sills, children skippin' up and down outside the shop. Even the men would sometimes come out of the pub with their pints to join in. Yeh know? . . . And when Terry got married that time The Cavalcaders sang at the weddin' mass. Terry actually left the altar and went up into the organ loft so the quartet could sing the Offertory that Eamon had written. 'We'll Bring You Water.' . . . Beautiful! . . .

Whatshisname was the best man that day – Rogan! He said in his speech after that Terry was probably the only man present who had ever sung at his own weddin'. 'And judgin' by the face of the bride when he left the altar,' says he, 'he was a lucky man not to be singin' at his own funeral too.' (BREDA *laughs*.) . . . That was probably the first time Terry ever left them alone together, yeh know – on the altar that day! Dangerous enough occupation too as it turned out.

NUALA. What was she like?

BREDA. Hah? Oh I don't know . . . She was a little bit like you – a little bit like me . . .

Pause. NUALA *loses herself in thought. The Cavalcaders are still singing in the background.* BREDA *looks up at* NUALA *and suddenly understands. Lights down. Lights rise on the shop.* TERRY *is sitting on the bench, dressed in his heavy overcoat. He is lost in thought. There is a loud rapping on the door.* TERRY *goes across and opens it.* RORY *enters with the bulb.*

TERRY. Did yeh get it?

RORY. Yeah . . . did that bulb go or what?

TERRY. Yeah.

RORY. Switch off that auld light there Terry, will yeh. . . . (*He climbs up onto the counter to change the bulb*.) . . . What are yeh wantin' to do about that auld piano?

TERRY. I don't know. What kind of shape is she in?

RORY. Oh I don't know. It sounds alright to me anyway.

TERRY *goes across to tinkle the piano.*

RORY. It's not too bad is it?

TERRY. What? No . . . Are you not wantin' to hang on to this for the young one?

RORY. Are yeh coddin' me or somethin'. Me mother 'd do her nut if I brought that yoke into the house. The state of it!

TERRY. I suppose I may hang on to it meself so. Although I'll probably be shot too. But sure . . . This came out of our little kitchen yeh know. Hard to believe, ain't it? The whole street was out the day they rolled it down the hill here to the shop – me uncle Eamon and big Tom Nail and all. Meself and Josie were only little lads at the time – taggin' along behind and that – me poor Ma peerin' out from behind the little half door. A half door be Jaysus! Anyone 'd think I was talkin' about a hundred years ago or somethin'! The poor crator was so ashamed of herself that she became just a little face in that auld dark doorway in the end. Practically disappeared, she did. Yeh know I can hardly even remember her dyin'. I mean, if it wasn't for me uncle Eamon I'd 've been lost altogether. Yeh know Communions and Confirmations and all the rest of it. Sure he worked wonders with me really when I think of it – considerin' like!

RORY. Aye? . . . That's her now.

He climbs down and goes across to switch on the light.

But sure maybe it'll start yeh composin' again Terry if nothin' else hah? Remember that night? Stop the noise says you! . . . Jaysus they were innocent auld days though Terry weren't they? Hah?

TERRY. Yeah well, they could have been.

RORY. What?

Suddenly TERRY's head whips round and he looks towards the back room doorway, terror in his eyes.

What 's up?

TERRY 'Vhat? Nothin' . . . Jaysus it's warm in here ain't it?

RORY. What?

TERRY (*mopping his brow*). I 'm sweatin'.

RORY. You're leakin' boy! . . . Are yeh alright Terry?

TERRY nods.

RORY looks into TERRY's eyes, a little concerned. Then he goes into the back room.

TERRY. They say her face was bone white when they found her yeh know . . .

RORY (*off*). Who 's that?

TERRY. Hah?

RORY (*peeping out*). Did you say somethin'?

TERRY grimaces and turns away. RORY eyes him suspiciously and exits. Lights down. Lights rise on the shop. JOSIE and TED are present, dressed in their stage suits – blazers, black pants, white frilly shirts and bow ties. JOSIE's outfit is in disarray, the bow tie open, etc. TED is changing into his street clothes. RORY's stage suit is hanging up close by. JOSIE opens a bottle of Guinness just as RORY enters with a handful of dripping mugs.

RORY. I wonder what's keepin' the other fella? He was talkin' to your man Poe as I was comin' down the stairs of the hall.

I think he was gettin' another bookin' off of him or somethin'. He's a queer dour lookin' man though ain't he? Poe!

JOSIE. That's for sure.

RORY. He's well named anyway.

JOSIE. Yeah. He's a Poe by name and nature.

RORY. Somethin' queer happened to him when he was young or somethin' didn't it?

JOSIE. Yeah. He found his Da dead down in the cellar – lyin' in a pool of blood. Seemly he walked into the side of a coffin. Hit him right there in the temple. A little pool of blood not the size of your nail they say.

RORY. Jaysus hah? . . . Deep in the dungeon?

JOSIE. Yeah – where the sun don't shine!

RORY *thinks about it all.*

RORY. I don't think Terry'll be over the moon about the way things went tonight do you?

JOSIE. I wouldn't think so, no. But sure what can yeh do? I mean to say they're entitled to sing whatever they want.

RORY. All the same though Josie . . . Are yeh wantin' a coffee Ted?

TED. No thanks.

RORY. Three of our numbers they ripped off. Or was it four?

JOSIE. Three from tonight's programme. Four if you include 'Monday Monday', but sure we weren't goin' to do that tonight anyway.

RORY. Jaysus it was really panic stations there for a while though wasn't it? Hah? (*He laughs.*) Terry was goin' mad tryin' to change the programme round.

JOSIE. 'Oh Lord Jaysus,' says he, 'there's another one gone.' No but the thing that amuses me though is that meself and Terry have been on this group for over twenty years now and we still only know about twenty-five songs – if we're lucky!

RORY. Were you up in my house this evenin' Ted?

TED. Yeah.

RORY. Well?

TED. Ah I didn't get a whole lot done. I hadn't a lot of time after. I made a start on it. I'll go up tomorrow evenin' and get stuck into them.

RORY. Good. I'll have somewhere to hang me hat at long last . . . Jaysus it was a fairly bad auld show all round tonight though lads wasn't it? Where does he get them eh? I'd say he makes a fair few bob out of it, yeh know. He went home in the hearse. His wife was like Morticia in the back! (*He sniggers.*) . . . 'Frank McCarthy the well known memory man and clair-voyant,' says he, 'will not be appearin' due to unforeseen circumstances.' And did yeh ever see anything like that ventriloquist. Read my lips hah!

JOSIE. That's what I say, but sure what can yeh do.

TERRY (*entering*). Did yeh ever see anything like that in all your born days did yeh? Hah?

JOSIE. What?

TERRY. Do yeh know what I call that now? Plagiarism of the highest order, that's what I call that boy!

JOSIE. But sure they're entitled to sing those songs if they want to. I mean to say we didn't write them or anything.

TERRY. They're entitled to sing whatever songs they want, yeah, but they don't have to rip us off do they? I mean to say they must have knocked off five or six of our numbers there tonight.

JOSIE. Four if yeh include, 'Monday Monday', but sure we weren't goin to do that anyway.

TERRY. Three of our barber shop songs they did. The very same arrangements and all. The same hand movements and everything!

JOSIE. Yeah well, yeh don't need to be Marcel Marceau to figure them out, now do yeh?

TERRY. It's a wonder they didn't have the same suits as us and all and they at it.

JOSIE. Are yeh coddin' me or what?

TERRY. What's that supposed to mean?

RORY. Yeah Josie, what's wrong with them?

JOSIE. We're like four fuckin' waiters goin' around.

TERRY. We're supposed to be like four waiters ain't we?

JOSIE. Are we?

TERRY. Yes, we are.

JOSIE. Oh!

RORY. Yeah, so don't mock the afflicted boy! But sure yeh know what they say Terry, imitation is a form of flattery.

TERRY. A form of heart attack too. I said it to your man Poe afterwards, mind yeh. I mean to say puttin' them on earlier on in the show would have been bad enough but puttin' them on directly before us was absolutely cat melodian altogether.

JOSIE. What did he say?

TERRY. He said he didn't know what they were goin' to do. To tell yeh the truth he wasn't that put out about it.

RORY. Downtown Munich hah!

JOSIE. Is that what they were called?

TERRY. Downtown Mimic'd be more like it.

JOSIE. Did your man give yeh another bookin'?

TERRY. Yeah. Two weeks' time. So hang up those suits properly after yez. We don't want to be havin' to get them cleaned again between this and then . . . The only thing is, this other crowd are goin' to be on the same bill.

JOSIE. Well I was just sayin' to the lads here a few minutes ago the thing I don't understand is you and me must be on this group this twenty years or more and we still only know about twenty-five songs.

TERRY. Yeah well we'll have a few new babies on the agenda the next time we go out I don't mind tellin' yeh.

JOSIE. Yeah? Three years' work in a fortnight be Jaysus!

RORY. Anythin' in mind Terry?

TERRY. We're goin' to write a few numbers ourselves.

JOSIE. Yeh what?

TERRY. We done it before didn't we with 'One Heart Broken'?

JOSIE. Yeah but we had your uncle Eamon to write the music that time though, didn't we.

TERRY. I wrote the words . . . But sure there's a chap there and he's trained in composition (*He means* TED.)

JOSIE. Yeah – 'A Day At The Seaside!' . . . What's wrong with you anyway, you're very quiet?

TED. What? Nothin'.

JOSIE *eyes him suspiciously.*

RORY. That's a good idea though Terry – a couple of original numbers!

TERRY. What?

JOSIE. What are yeh goin' to write about?

TERRY. What do yeh mean, what am I goin' to write about? Take a look out the window any day of the week and you'll find somethin' to write about. A whole universe of stuff out there and he's wonderin' what we're goin' to write about. I don't know!

JOSIE. All I ever hear any of yez talkin' about is Legs Eleven from the bank goin' by.

RORY. Beautiful Bundoran hah! She was at the concert tonight too. Sittin' in the third row she was with her legs crossed – nearly put me off a couple of times I don't mind tellin' yeh.

JOSIE. Was that what it was?

TERRY. Yeh know the more I think about how cool that fella took my complaint there tonight!

JOSIE. Who's that?

TERRY. Whatshisname, Poe!

RORY. By name and nature! He buried me Da there last year, yeh know.

TERRY. Yeah well, he won't be buryin' me then I don't mind tellin' yeh. A big face on him now like a well slapped arse, the same fella.

RORY. He cut all his wife's hair off one time or somethin', didn 't he?

TERRY. Yeah. he was goin' off to some convention or somethin' and he was afraid of his life that she'd go out on the rantan while he was away and he cut all her hair off.

JOSIE. Oh by name and nature boy! Are you headin' over for one Ted?

TED. No, I'm goin' to head on up the hill home.

JOSIE. What? There must be a blue moon out there tonight or somethin', is there?

RORY. I'll come over for one with yeh, Josie.

JOSIE. What?

RORY. Are yeh goin' over for one, Terry?

TERRY. No.

RORY. What?

JOSIE (singing). Blue Moon Of Kentucky Keep On Shinin'. . .

RORY. Terry is already composin', are yeh? Inspiration hah?

JOSIE. Perspiration 'd be more like it now I'd say .

RORY. Hey Josie, hang up that suit properly after yeh, will yeh.

JOSIE. It's alright.

RORY. It's not alright.

JOSIE (*mockingly*). It's not alright.

TERRY. Give that other thing a bit of thought though, Ted, will yeh? I mean if we're goin' to move on it we'd nearly need to be doin' somethin' soon like, yeh know.

TED. Yeah alright. I have a couple of chord sequences goin' round in me head alright.

RORY. Lennon and McCartney look out.

JOSIE. Yeah. Bill and Ben, the flowerpot men. Come on.

The three of them leave. Pause. TERRY goes across and switches on and off the light three times. He goes and sits up on the counter and waits. Lights down. Lights rise on the shop. TERRY, dressed in his vest and pants, is lying prone along the counter, a couple of cushions at his back. His shirt and jumper and coat etc are strewn about the place along with some of NUALA's clothing. He is leafing his way through a child's copy book. We hear NUALA speaking off and soon she enters, in her slip and bare footed.

NUALA. The Pelican is the noblest bird of them all, yeh know. She sacrifices herself for her young. Yeh see when her chilbren are born and begin to grow up they flap about and beat their wings and that and they hit the mother and father in the face all the time until one of them becomes angry and strikes them back and accidentally kills them. After that the mother sort of mourns for a few days and then on the third day she'll pierce her breast and open her side and she'll lay across her little babes, pouring out her blood all over the dead bodies and this brings them back to life again. That's what my poem is all about, yeh see. The Noble Pelican! . . . River Reddens. Swan Serene. Wonders As She Wanders Through The Dead Of Night. Blood Soaked Morning Stains The Day. As Two Dead Babes Come Out To Play . . . But sure there's another one in there about the Rowan Tree. The Rowan Tree is supposed to possess some sort of mystical powers, yeh know, to ward off evil spirits or somethin'. When I was young we used to have one growin' up around the house. Its branches touched my little bedroom window. Made me feel really safe – like I was sleepin' in the arms of a big gentle giant or somethin'. Our house used to look out on an auld spooky graveyard like, yeh know? Are yeh alright?

TERRY. Yeah.

She takes his hand.

NUALA. You've cut yourself again.

TERRY. What?

NUALA. You've cut yourself. Why don't yeh wear the gloves I gave yeh.

TERRY. I do sometimes.

NUALA. I wish yeh would. (*She kisses his hand.*) I really wish yeh would . . . What are yeh thinkin' about?

TERRY. Nothin'.

NUALA. Yeh never talk to me, Terry. Yeh never tell me anythin'.

TERRY. I tell yeh all yeh need to know.

NUALA. Yeah but yeh don't say the things I need to hear though, do yeh? I'm crazy about you, yeh know. You're the love of my life. I mean it. I love yeh Terry . . . Did yeh hear what I said to yeh?

TERRY *sighs, rises and begins to dress.*

Yeh treat me so cruel sometimes, Terry. Yeh really do.

TERRY. Jesus Nuala, stop will yeh, and don't start.

NUALA. What's that supposed to mean?

TERRY. What's it supposed to mean? In all the time that you've been comin' over here did yeh ever once hear me say that word?

NUALA. What word?

TERRY. You know what word.

NUALA. Love?

TERRY. Yeah. Did yeh ever hear me say it? (*She shakes her head.*) Did yeh ever hear me mention it – or hint it even? Yeh didn't, did yeh? (*She shakes her head.*) Right. I mean to say you can say it all yeh want. It's your prerogative. Maybe it makes yeh feel good or somethin'. I don't know. Or maybe you need to find justification for all this. But I don't, yeh see.

NUALA. I say it because it's true.

TERRY. No. You say it because yeh want to hear the words reverberatin' back to yeh. You think you're up in the Alps or somewhere. Well you're not in the Alps. You're in the lowlands lows girl – the same as meself!

NUALA. If I thought you didn't love me I swear I think I'd . . .

TERRY. What?

NUALA. I don't know. I'd throw meself off the bridge or somethin'.

TERRY. Now do yeh hear that – that's the very kind of thing now that . . . Do yeh know somethin', I ought to give yeh a back hander for that, that's what I should do. I mean look at yeh. Hangdog! You're twenty-two years of age for Jaysus sake! I'm nearly twice your age and I feel younger than you do.

NUALA. I've given yeh so much, Terry. I've given yeh everythin'. I've poured out my soul to yeh and I hardly know anythin' about you.

TERRY. Well what exactly is it yeh need to know?

NUALA. I don't know.

TERRY. What?

NUALA. I need to know what she looks like.

TERRY. What?

NUALA. Your wife?

TERRY. What about her?

NUALA. I've been told that yeh still carry a photo of her with yeh in your wallet everywhere yeh go.

TERRY. Who told yeh that?

NUALA. Is it true?

TERRY. What if it is?

NUALA. I want to know what she looks like.

TERRY. Why?

NUALA. Because I just need to know that's all.

TERRY. Oh yeh just need to know! Jesus . . . God, give me patience!

NUALA. I found out where she lives, yeh know . . . I found out where she lives and I went to her house to see her.

TERRY. When?

NUALA. One day last week.

TERRY. How did yeh get up there?

NUALA. Took a train.

TERRY. Are you mad or what?

NUALA. Don't say that to me Terry . . . It's alright, yeh needn't worry, I didn't go near her or anything. I just hung around outside the house for a few hours that's all.

TERRY. Yeh didn t see her then?

NUALA *shakes her head sulkily*.

Nobody home?

NUALA. Some fella on a walkin' stick . . . But I do need to know what she looks like though Terry, yeh know. I mean I really need to know what I'm up against.

TERRY. Oh yeh need to know what you're up against! That's different. Why didn't yeh say so. I mean if yeh need to know what you're up against! Well I mean . . .

NUALA. What?

TERRY. Hah? . . . Jesus! (*He paces about irritably.*) Right! Alright. Here. (*Angrily he takes out a photo and forces it upon her.*) Here. There. Now. Now yeh know. Are yeh happy now? Hah? Yeah? Happy? . . . Now do you think for one minute that you can compete against that. Do you seriously think for one minute that you can compete . . .

NUALA. That picture's nearly twenty years old. She don't look like that any more.

TERRY. That's not what I asked yeh. Do yeh think you can compete against it, is what I'm askin' yeh.

NUALA. Yeah I do.

TERRY. How?

NUALA. Easy.

TERRY. How easy?

NUALA. What?

TERRY. How easy, I said. Hah?

NUALA *, in a fit of rage, snatches the photograph from his hand and tears it in two, throwing it on the floor.* TERRY *takes her by the hair and slings her to the ground. He bends to pick up the pieces.*

TERRY. Don't you ever touch anythin' belongin' to me again.

NUALA. She don't look like that now.

TERRY. You're fuckin' neurotic, yeh know. A feckin' fruit cake yeh are.

NUALA. Well at least I'm not walkin' around in someone else's shadow all the time, anyway.

TERRY. What's that supposed to mean?

NUALA. He took her away from you and now you're takin' it out on me. But I'm not the one who needs to be forgiven . . .

TERRY. Do yeh know somethin', all those head shrinkers you're goin' to are beginnin' to take effect on yeh, I think.

NUALA. Because I'm not the one who hurt yeh. I didn't do yeh any wrong Terry . . .

TERRY. But if you're goin' to start analysin' anybody then I'd prefer if yeh picked somebody else, if yeh don't mind. preferably somewhere else . . .

NUALA. Maybe yeh need to forgive yourself for callin' him a friend in the first place.

TERRY. You don't know nothin' about it.

NUALA. I know . . . I know . . .

TERRY. What do yeh know? What is it yeh know?

NUALA. I know that he was supposed to be your best friend and he let yeh down – stole your wife away from yeh, moved in with her above the little baker's shop right across the street there.

TERRY. Ain't that awful what I've to listen to, too . . .

NUALA. And it used to break your heart to have to stand here and look at the two of them goin' in and out every day, holdin' hands and talkin' and laughin' and lookin' at one another and all . . .

TERRY. Two weeks in a funny farm and she thinks she's a professor or somethin'.

NUALA. But he didn't give a toss about you – not a toss. Of course you thought the sun, moon and stars shone out of him. Rogan could do no wrong as far as you were concerned. Rogan did this and Rogan did that and Rogan did the other thing and everybody knows he never did nothin' really. While you were walkin' the slippy pole and swimmin' the river or runnin' races he was standin' there like a duke in blue jeans be Jaysus lookin' at himself in a shop window. A real little shite goin' around if yeh ask me. Couldn't even get his own girl!

TERRY. Oh, you'd know, of course.

NUALA. But unfortunately he 's not goin' to bring her back to yeh Terry. I 'm sorry to have to be the one to inform yeh and all but . . .

TERRY. The day I need a headbanger like you to tell me how to live my life . . .

NUALA. She's not comin' back to yeh Terry.

TERRY. Is the day I'll lie down and . . .

NUALA. She's not comin' back boy. Yeh may forget about her. She's not comin' back .

TERRY. I know she's not comin' back.

NUALA. Well what are yeh waitin' for then? Hah? What are yeh waitin' for?

TERRY. If you think now for one minute that I'm goin' to stand here and listen to you bullshittin' . . .

NUALA. What are yeh waitin' for?

TERRY. What am I waitin' for? I'll tell yeh what I'm waitin' for. Do yeh want to know what I'm waitin' for? I'm waitin' for you to get the f . . .

Red with rage, hands clenched TERRY *looks around for something to vent his spleen on.* NUALA *watches him calmly. When his rage has passed he stands breathless, holding on to the counter.* NUALA *moves towards him with tender eyes.*

NUALA. I'm the other half of you Terry, you're the other half of me!

TERRY *sighs, chuckling through his exasperation.*

TERRY. I don't think you should come over here any more, Nuala.

NUALA. What?

TERRY. I'm no good for yeh . . . I'm only usin' yeh, sure!

NUALA. Usin' me? What do yeh mean – usin' me?

TERRY. What are yeh wantin' me to do, spell it out for yeh or somethin'? . . . Don't look at me like that. It gives me the creeps when yeh look at me like that. I mean to say that's the very thing now that . . . Look I'm old and you're young. You need somebody young – someone who'll talk to yeh and all, tell yeh things. You need help! Yeh should be able to see through fellas like me anyway. I mean to say, Jesus Christ, I'm practically whatdoyoucallit . . .

NUALA. What do yeh mean, 'usin' me?'

TERRY. Usin' yeh, usin' yeh! I'm only usin' yeh!

TERRY *looks into her fawn-like eyes.*

Look Nuala. Look.

She breaks away.

NUALA. I'm a person, Terry. There's a person inside of me.

TERRY. I know you're a person. if I didn't think there was – a person inside of yeh, I wouldn't be tellin' yeh not to come over here any more now, would I? Hah? Now would I?

NUALA. If I thought I'd never see you again I think I'd die.

TERRY. Yeh won't die at all.

NUALA. I would. Give us a chance, Terry. I'll do anythin'.

TERRY. There's no point, Nuala. We've already done everything worth talkin' about and it just don't seem to make any difference. I mean I just don't feel anythin' for yeh like, yeh know. It's not your fault. It's mine. I mean I don't really feel anythin' for anybody anymore yeh know. I mean . . . Ah I don't know . . . Look, just take your things will yeh and go. Go on and don't come over here again.

NUALA. What? (TERRY *turns away from her*.) I have things to offer, Terry. I mean I'm worthy of . . . I mean . . . I'm a worthy person . . . I mean Breda says that he was only a little shit too, yeh know – couldn't even get his own girl!

TERRY. Breda! (*He sniggers softly*.)

NUALA. I know you're really a nice fella at heart, Terry. I know yeh are.

TERRY. I'm not. At heart, or on the surface, or any other way, I'm not a nice fella . I'm not!

NUALA. What?

TERRY. Believe me Nuala, I'm not!

NUALA. I could help yeh to forget about her though Terry, yeh know.

TERRY. What?

NUALA. I said I could help yeh to forget about her.

TERRY. Go ahead home Nuala, will yeh. Go on, get out of here. And stay away from here altogether in the future.

NUALA. You don't really mean that Terry.

TERRY. What?

NUALA. You don't mean that.

TERRY. What is wrong with you eh? I mean where's your pride? Don't you have any pride? I'm tryin' to dump yeh here, and here you are standin' there like an ejit takin' it all. I mean where's your pride, girl? Hah? Hah? I mean, Jesus! . . . Hello, is there anybody in there? Hah?

NUALA. Why are yeh doin' this, Terry?

TERRY. Look, just get out of my life, will yeh. Go on, beat it . . .

NUALA. What?

TERRY. What? What? What? Yeh should see yourself there. You're like a fuckin' puppet on a string or somethin'. The big bulgin' eyes on yeh! So? What?

NUALA. What? To tell yeh the truth Terry, I'm half afraid to go. I mean if I go . . .

TERRY. If yeh go, yeh go. So go!

NUALA. What? Where?

TERRY. What do I care. I mean I don't care where yeh go, do I. Just go. Back to your Da's farm or somewhere. Back to the funny farm if yeh like. I mean I don't care. It makes no odds to me one way or another where you go or don't go, because you don't mean doodle shit to me like, yeh know. I mean I swear I don't give you one second thought from one end of the day to the next. Yeh know? Doodle shit! That's all you are to me.

NUALA. What?

TERRY (*mimics her*). What?

NUALA *suddenly grabs her things and flees tearfully, banging the door behind her.* TERRY *stares towards the doorway. He sighs. Pause.*

God forgive me.

Lights down. Lights rise on the shop. Night. TED *is sitting at the piano.* JOSIE *is sitting on a stool in the middle of the shop, shining The Cavalcaders' shoes.*

JOSIE. I wouldn't mind but everything was goin' grand until Terry's uncle Eamon found his wife out in the hotel yard in the arms of another man and he threw off his coat and went bald-headed for the pair of them. Meself and Terry had to go out after him to try and calm him down. And then when we got back inside here was your man Rogan dancin' with the bride, glidin' around the floor and she gazin' up into his eyes and all. I'm not coddin' yeh, yeh could nearly smell the treachery in the air, boy! I go into the bar then and I overhear the Bullet O' Brien passin' some remark about Terry's ma and I reared up cat melodian on him . . . Jaysus, it was some weddin', boy!

TED. Why, what did he say about her, like?

JOSIE. What? Ah the usual, yeh know. 'Wait 'til I see now,' says
   he, 'it was either a journey man piano tuner who got her into
   trouble or some sleazy lookin' banjo player on an auld
   travellin' dance band. Either way,' says he, 'Terry was destined
   to be a fairly musical bastard whichever way it went.' . . .
   I asked the Bullet O'Brien outside and everything over that
   day, yeh know. The two of us bet the shit out of one another
   up at the back of the C.Y. Stop the noise boy! War there was!
   (*He chuckles.*)

TED. What did yeh make of her?

JOSIE. Who's that? Terry's missus?

TED. Yeah. I mean did yeh think she was a bit of a whore like –
   goin' off with your man like that in the end?

JOSIE. A whore? No. Ah no, it was nothin' like that or anythin'.
   I mean she wasn't like Eamon's missus or anythin' like, yeh
   know . . . She was a queer good lookin' woman though.

TED. Yeah?

JOSIE. Oh yeah. She used to often come in here after they were
   married. She'd sit up at that auld counter there – the sun
   streamin' through her hair . . . Jaysus there'd be more botched
   up jobs after she was gone boy, I'm not coddin' yeh. Poor auld
   Eamon used to nearly do his nut, that's all. I wouldn't mind, but
   they say she lives like a nun now. I believe she rarely goes out
   any more. She tends the garden all the time and nurses him like
   a nun. You'd hardly think it was the same woman I believe. Or
   man! What's wrong with yeh?

TED. What? . . . Ah nothin'. I'll tell yeh after.

   TERRY *enters from the back room.*

TERRY. I got it Ted. Play us that F Minor again there, will yeh.

TED. What?

TERRY. If Josie sings it straight, right. And you go . . . What is
   it? . . . It's Sayonara Street. We've Come This Far . Da Da Da
   Da Da . . . G Sharp Minor . . . Da Da Da Da Da . Goodbye . . .
   Yeh know?

TED. Yeah.

TERRY. Rory stays where he was and I'll go da da da . . . Or
   whatever. Yeh know? What do yeh think?

   RORY *enters with a parcel of fish and chips.*

TED. Yeah . . . Maybe . . .

TERRY. We let it flow then into . . . da da da da . . . Yeh know?

And you don't forget to open up your lungs on that change.

TED *nods and begins to jot it down musically.*

JOSIE. What? . . . Yeah . . .

RORY. Stella has a new sign up in the chipper. KNIVES AND FORKS ARE NOT MEDICINE AND SHOULD NOT BE TAKEN AFTER MEALS . . . (*He doles out the fish and chips.*)

JOSIE. Where's me change?

RORY. What? (*He makes a fist at him.*)

TERRY. Good . . . Well Rory, did yeh ask her?

RORY. Yeah.

TERRY. Is she comin' over?

RORY. Yeah, she'll be over in a minute. Listen whatshername is standin' over in the shop doorway too – Nuala! Do yeh want me to ask her over as well or what?

TERRY. What?

RORY. I mean to say, the more the merrier like, yeh know.

TED. Ah no, just leave it at Breda I think.

RORY. What?

TERRY. Yeah, leave it.

RORY. What do you think, Josie?

JOSIE (*eating*). It's immaterial to me.

RORY. Alright.

The men take a break to eat their fish and chips.

TERRY. Are yeh alright, Ted?

TED. Yeah.

JOSIE. Are you still alright for tomorrow?

RORY. Yeah. What time are yeh wantin' to go at?

JOSIE. Oh ten'll do yeh.

RORY. Right. You be down here at ten to ten.

TERRY. What's that?

RORY. I've to drop Josie up to the hospital tomorrow mornin'.

TERRY. What for?

JOSIE. Ah they're goin to do a few auld tests on me.

TERRY. Well thanks for tellin' me.

JOSIE. Why, what are yeh wantin' to do, come up and hold me hand or somethin'?

TERRY. No, but it'd be nice to know these things, that's all. Go into a pub and somebody asks me how yeh are or somethin', and I haven't a clue what they're talkin' about.

JOSIE. It's only a couple of tests they're doin'. Stop fussin,' will yeh.

TERRY. I'm not fussin' at all. I'd just like to know these things.

JOSIE. Yeah well, now yeh know.

BREDA *enters*.

Here she is now . . . The one and only.

TERRY. How are yeh, Breda. Get Breda a stool there Rory, will yeh.

BREDA. What?

RORY. Right.

BREDA. What is this, a private audience or somethin'?

TERRY. Yeah, somethin' like that, Breda.

JOSIE. Well you're more like a guinea pig really Breda, yeh know.

BREDA. Thanks very much, Josie.

RORY. That's nice Breda, ain't it? Hah? Here y'are hon, sit down there and lig do scí . . . Do yeh want me to take off her shoes or anythin', Terry?

BREDA. Me shoes are alright where they are . . .

RORY. Hey, that reminds me, I'm not talkin' to you anyway.

BREDA. Why, what did I do now?

RORY. Runnin' around with French men!

BREDA. What?

JOSIE. I was tellin' him about your man Jacques – the French fella who used to come home to Breens every summer.

BREDA. Oh yeah – Jacques LePouvier, hah! I wonder whatever happened to him.

JOSIE. He's probably in the French Foreign Legion or somewhere, Breda.

RORY. You were mad about him anyway – accordin' to Josie.

BREDA. You must be jokin' me.

JOSIE. All the girls were after him, boy.

BREDA. I'd be made up with him now – a little short arse goin' around.

JOSIE. You wouldn't have said that if yeh had to box him, Breda. Jaysus, he was a lovely boxer boy! Wasn't he, Terry?

TERRY. Yeah. He was good alright.

RORY. Bon jour, yeh whore, tonight for sure hah!

JOSIE. Yeah . . . Are yeh wantin' a few chips, Breda?

BREDA. No thanks.

TERRY. I would've loved to 've seen Rogan taken him on though, yeh know. That would've been a right fight, boy!

JOSIE. Yeah, I wouldn't've minded seein' that one meself, mind yeh.

TERRY. What?

JOSIE. Jacques would've killed him.

TERRY. I don't know Josie! I mean Rogan was hard too, yeh know. And he was queer fast boy!

JOSIE. He had no heart though.

TERRY. Are yeh coddin' me, or what. Rogan was afraid of nothin' or no one, boy!

JOSIE. Jacques would have cut him to ribbons.

TERRY. Yeah well, you didn't know him like I did, Josie.

BREDA *sighs and exits to the back room.*

JOSIE. He was only a bum.

TERRY. What do yeh mean he was only a bum?

JOSIE. He was only a bum. He let everyone down.

TERRY. He didn't let everyone down. He let me down.

JOSIE. Same thing.

TERRY. Anyway who are we to talk, after what we done.

JOSIE. That was different.

TERRY. What was different about it? There was nothin' different about it, Josie!

JOSIE. It was different. We were only young fellas and we only did it the once and then we copped on to yourselves.

TERRY. Yeah, too late for poor old Eamon, though.

JOSIE. Once!

RORY. Jaysus, even Our Lord fell three times lads.

JOSIE *glares at* RORY *and then turns to* TERRY.

JOSIE. What are yeh always harpin' on about that for, anyway?
You're always harpin' on about that!

TERRY. I'm not always harpin' on about it at all. I'm just pointin'
out to yeh that what he done and what we done was no
different, that's all.

JOSIE. I mean, what about her. I mean. She was no saint or
anythin'. And your uncle Eamon knew that too, and he should
have kept his eye on her. I mean we were only two young
fellahs. Jesus Christ, I mean! . . . (*He sighs and angrily rolls his
food up into a paper ball. He rises and goes behind the counter
in search of a waste basket.*) I don't know!

TERRY. What?

JOSIE. Nothin'. Forget it.

TERRY. Huh?

JOSIE. Look, forget it, will yeh.

*He wipes the grease from his hands and goes behind the
counter. Silence.* BREDA *returns with a cup of water. She pops
a pill.*

RORY. Are you workin' late tonight Breda, yeah?

BREDA. Yeah . . . What am I'm goin' to hear now, anyway?

RORY. Two new songs, Breda. The first two numbers written for
and by The Cavalcaders since 'One Heart Broken'.

BREDA. Yeah? What are they called?

RORY. The first one is called, 'When The Sheets Are Shorter The
Bed Looks Longer'. And the second one is entitled, 'No Matter
How Far A Fish Swims You'll Never See Him Sweat.'

TED. Yeh can't beat the auld jokes Breda, can yeh?

BREDA. No.

TERRY. Right . . . would yeh like a cup of tea or anythin' Breda,
while you're . . .

BREDA. Look, just get on with it, will yeh. I've a woman over
there under a dryer and if I don't get her out fairly soon she's
goin' to explode on me.

TERRY. Oh right . . . We're all a little bit nervous now. That's
why we want to try the new numbers out on you before we go
up to the concert tomorrow night like, yeh know.

JOSIE *enters*.

BREDA. I know all of that. Come on.

TERRY. OK. Are yeh alright, Ted?

TED. Yeah.

TERRY. Alright, fire away, so.

BREDA. Oh, hang on for Nuala.

TERRY. What?

BREDA. Nuala's comin' over. (BREDA *rises and goes to the door to call across the street*.) Nuala! Nuala! Come on . . . She's comin'. She's just shuttin' up the shop.

RORY. Whenever you're ready now, Breda.

BREDA. What? She's comin' . . . But sure, yeh can tell me the history behind the songs while we're waitin', how yeh came to write them and all?

TERRY. What they're about, yeh mean?

BREDA. Yeah.

TERRY. Well the first song I suppose is a sort of a love song. And the second one . . . I suppose it's a sort of a love song too really, ain't it?

TED. Yeah.

BREDA. Two love songs.

RORY. Queer imaginative Breda, ain't we? Hah? (*He chuckles*.)

BREDA. Mmn . . .

RORY. The truth of the matter is Breda, the first song is about Legs Eleven from the bank who goes by here every day, and the second one is about this fella who's tryin' to wriggle his way out of an affair. That's called Sayonara Street. 'Here We Are', says he, 'It's Sayonara Street. We've Come This Far And Now We Are Complete. It's Sayonara Street. Goodbye.' Simple as that! Come in Nuala.

NUALA *enters*.

TERRY. How are yeh, Nuala? Get Nuala a stool there Rory, will yeh. Have we any more stools left?

RORY. What do yeh think we're runnin' here, a picture house or somethin'? Sit up on the counter there, Nuala. Hey Terry, give her a couple of those cushions there. I'm like a butler here. Pierre hah! LePompidou! . . . Lie down there, Nuala .

NUALA. What?

NUALA *props herself up with cushions. She looks lovely.*
TERRY *can't take his eyes off of her. He picks up an extra*
cushion and brings it to her.

TERRY. There y'are, Nuala. Put that at your back hon . . . Did you
change your hair style or somethin', Nuala? It looks sort of
different or somethin'.

NUALA. What? No, I just didn't bother to put it up this mornin',
that's all.

TERRY. It's lovely then. It really suits her like that, Breda, don't
it?

BREDA. Yeah. You've a grand bit of hair, Nuala.

NUALA. Thanks.

Silence.

TED. Are yez right, or what?

TERRY. What? Oh yeah, right Ted. Let her go. You don't forget
what I was sayin' to yeh, now.

JOSIE. Yeah, yeah, come on will yeh.

TERRY. Right Ted.

TED *plays the introduction. They sing.*

SONG. Hey Mister, did yeh see that girl.
She walks around like she owned the world
You'd think she owned the world.

Hey sister, did yeh see that girl
Her head's so high you'd swear she owned the sky
You'd think she owned the sky.

I only wish I knew what day it was
So I could tell her exactly the way it was
Or the way that it could be between her and me.

Hey Mister, did yeh see that girl
She walks around like she owned the world
You'd think she owned the world.

Lights down.

ACT TWO

Lights rise on the shoe shop. It is morning. TED *and* RORY *are working behind the counter.* TERRY *is busy pottering around the place, taking stock, etc.*

RORY. No sign of Beautiful Bundoran at the concert at all last night Terry, hah?

TERRY. No.

RORY. We'll have to be excommunicatin' that one from the fan club I think. She didn't even give in a doctor's note or anything, did she?

TERRY. No. Not a word from her, boy!

RORY. After all the time and trouble we put into her, hah? That's the thanks we get now!

TERRY. Mmn . . .

RORY. There's that pile of shoes for the orphans, Terry, just in case that nun calls in for them while I'm out this mornin'.

TERRY. Right. I hope yeh built up the heels on them, did yeh?

RORY. Yeah.

TERRY. She likes to see high heels before she pays.

RORY. They are high. Sure look at them yourself there. They're like stilts . . . Jaysus the boys made a right show of themselves last night after though, didn't they? Hah?

TERRY. Who's that?

RORY. Downtown Munich.

TERRY. Oh stop.

RORY. The big fat lad fell off of the stage and everythin', he was that drunk. They started arguin' in the dressin' room after you were gone Ted, yeh know. The fella with the glasses kneed the big lad in the bollix and all. I'm not coddin' yeh, he went down like a ton of bricks, boy.

TERRY. But sure, it'll do wonders for his falsetto if nothin' else.

RORY. That's what Josie said too . . . Did you go straight home last night or what, Ted?

TED. Yeah. Ah I couldn't be bothered drinkin' last night. Listen,

I'll be back in a minute, Terry. I'm just wantin' to . . .

TERRY. What? Yeah right, Ted.

TED exits. RORY silently wonders about him. TERRY shrugs.

Oh yes, I think we can safely say that we wiped them fellas' eyes for 'em last night alright.

RORY. We saw 'em out of it alright didn't we? The two new numbers didn't go down too bad either, did they?

He exits to the back room.

TERRY. No, not too bad at all, mind yeh. A little more of the same now, I think.

NUALA enters. RORY returns for a tool.

RORY. How are yeh, Nuala?

NUALA. How are yeh.

TERRY. Nuala.

RORY. I didn t see yeh up at the show last night, Nuala.

NUALA. No, I didn't go.

RORY. Yeh missed it, then.

NUALA. Yeah?

RORY. Yeah. And you were missed too I don't mind tellin' yeh. Wasn't she, Terry?

TERRY. Yeah.

RORY exits to the back room again. NUALA steps up to the counter with a pair of boots to be mended.

TERRY. How are yeh doin'?

NUALA. Alright.

TERRY. That's good . . . I waited over here for yeh for a while last night, yeh know.

NUALA. Did yeh? . . . I noticed the light on, alright.

TERRY. Why didn't yeh come over?

NUALA. You told me not to.

TERRY. But sure yeh wouldn't want to be mindin' the things I'd say, Nuala. I'd say one thing one minute and the next I'd be . . . Yeh know yourself!

NUALA. All the same.

TERRY. Huh? . . . Look, I'm sorry if I said anything to hurt yeh or anythin'. I get kind of carried away with meself sometimes like, yeh know. I mean yeh know me? Listen Nuala, I really need to see yeh. Really . . . Will yeh come over here later on tonight?

NUALA. I don't know Terry. I don't think so.

TERRY. Why not?

NUALA. You're only usin' me, sure. Yeh said so yourself.

TERRY. Forget what I said, will yeh. Anyway what's all this 'usin' yeh' lark. So I'm usin' you and you're usin' me. I mean to say we're all usin' each another in one way or another.

NUALA. What do yeh mean? I'm not usin' you. I don't use people, Terry.

TERRY. Alright, alright . . . Look, come over to the shop tonight. I'll leave the light on as usual and . . .

NUALA. No. I can't.

TERRY. Why not?

NUALA. I just can't any more, that's all.

TERRY. What do yeh mean, yeh can't any more?

NUALA. I'm seein' someone else, Terry.

TERRY. What? Who?

NUALA. I'd rather not say.

TERRY. Why, is he married or somethin' . . . Do I know him? (*She nods.*) I know him! . . . By Jaysus, yeh don't let the grass grow under your feet, do yeh? So where did yeh meet him, then?

NUALA. He comes into the shop.

TERRY. He comes into the shop! I must know him then . . . I give up, who is it?

NUALA. I'd rather not say, Terry.

TERRY. Why not?

NUALA. Because he asked me not to.

TERRY. He asked yeh not to! Well how come I never saw yeh with anybody or anything? I mean where did yeh go with him like?

NUALA. I don't know. Out of town mostly.

TERRY. Why, does he have a car or somethin'?

NUALA. Sort of.

TERRY. What do yeh mean, sort of? He either has a car or he hasn't . . . And does he know about me?

NUALA. Yeah.

TERRY. Oh yeh told him about me . . . So he knows about me but I can't be told about him. And I know this geezer, do I? (NUALA *nods*.) . . . Well I must look like a right gobshite to him alright.

NUALA. It's not a competition, Terry.

TERRY. Yeah well, I'll tell yeh what we're goin' to do now. I'm goin' to wait over here for you tonight, right, and you needn't bother your arse comin' over at all unless you've given this fella the shove first. Right? I don t want to see yeh at all unless you've dumped him. And I want to know who he is too – and I don't care whether he's married or not. Now if yeh don't come over to see me tonight you can forget about it altogether 'cause we'll be finished as far as I'm concerned. Right? It's up to you. I mean to say I don't want to look like a gobshite at all. No way. Not in this town anyway. Yeh can take it or leave it, Nuala. I mean it makes no odds to me one way or another.

NUALA. Yeah, and then what Terry?

TERRY. What do yeh mean?

NUALA. What are we sneakin' around in the dark all the time for Terry? I'm not married , you're not married. I mean what are we hidin' all the time for?

TERRY. What are yeh talkin' about?

NUALA. Yeh never take me anywhere. We never go anywhere.

TERRY. Oh yeh want to go somewhere. Well where do yeh want to go. I mean where exactly is it yeh want to go?

NUALA. You haven't even told the other lads about me, have yeh. Because you're ashamed of me. You're ashamed to be seen with me.

TERRY. Look Nuala, you don't know this place like I do. I know this place.

NUALA. What's that supposed to mean?

TERRY. You're young and I'm old, that's all.

NUALA. What?

TERRY. What do yeh want from me Nuala? What do yeh want me to say?

NUALA. Nothin'. I just want to be wooed a little bit, Terry, that's all.

TERRY. Alright.So come over here tonight and I'll woo yeh all yeh want.

NUALA. Tch . . . I have to go .

TERRY. You've to go! (TERRY *sighs and scoffs to himself.*)

NUALA. I'm a person Terry. There's someone inside of me too, yeh know. (TERRY *shakes his head and sighs.*) . . . I'll see yeh.

She leaves in a huff just as TED *enters. The two men stand to watch her go.* TED *wonders about it.* RORY *returns.*

TERRY. I don 't know!

RORY. What's up, Terry.

TERRY *shakes his head and sighs.*

TERRY. Here, see what's wrong with them there, will yeh. (NUALA's *boots.*)

RORY. What's wrong with them? What's right with them, yeh mean! I mean, is she serious or what? Look at the state of them. (*He opens up the gaping hole and makes it sing.*) I Wander Down By That Little Babbling Brook. Its Every Ripple Speaks Of Thee . . .

TED. What were yeh sayin' to Nuala there, Terry?

TERRY. What? Nothin'. Why?

TED. Just wonderin'.

RORY. I don't know, lads .

TED *goes back to his bench.* TERRY *watches him suspiciously.*

I was just sayin' there though, Terry, that there was hardly anyone from around here at the concert last night, was there?

TERRY. There was no one from around here at it, sure. Bloody scandalous so it is! Jaysus in the auld days this whole neighbourhood 'd be flockin' in to see The Cavalcaders, so they would.

RORY. Aye?

TERRY. Oh yeah. The Cavalcaders! Stop the noise! But sure when me uncle Eamon wrote the mass that time, the little chapel was burstin' at the seams with people. They were standin' out on the street and everything. And every one of them as proud as punch about it. You'd swear they were after writin' it themselves or somethin'. There was some great characters around here that time though, yeh know. Not like now. There's no real charac- ters around now. A fella turns his hat back to front or somethin' now and they all think he's a great fella . . . Me uncle Eamon was like a god around here that time though, yeh know. They'd nearly get off the path for him, man. Until she got her hands on him, of course. By Jaysus she really sapped the magic out of him alright, boy.

RORY. How do yeh mean?

TERRY. What?

TED *goes out to the back room.* TERRY *watches him. Pause.*

RORY. Jaysus, it'd be great to have that kind of support now though, Terry, wouldn't it? Hah? They stay away in their droves now, don't they? Afraid of their lives that they might enjoy themselves of course, ain't they? Hah?

TERRY. Mmn . . . Does Ted ever ask you for a loan of your car this weather?

RORY. What? Yeah, sometimes yeah. Why?

TERRY. No reason. Just wonderin'.

RORY. What?

JOSIE *enters, a bag in his hand.*

RORY. Wha-hoo . . . (*He sings.*) Bags packed and all boy hah! . . . Are yeh all set, yeah?

JOSIE. Yeah.

RORY. Yeh won't know him the next time yeh see him, Terry.

TERRY. How's that?

RORY. What? They're goin' to do a bit of an exploration job on him.

TERRY. How do yeh mean?

RORY. A magical mystery tour on his innards.

TERRY. What? I thought yeh were only goin' in for a few tests.

JOSIE. Yeah well, yeh know what Thought done, don't yeh?

RORY. Yeah. He pissed in his pants and Thought he was sweatin'.

TERRY. How long will yeh be in for?

JOSIE. I don't know. A couple of weeks, I suppose.

TERRY. But sure I thought yeh were only goin' in for the mornin' – that you'd be home by dinner hour. It's a good job I didn't take any more bookin's for the group then, ain't it.

JOSIE. That's all he's worried about.

TERRY. Yeah well, it'd be nice to be told about these things like, yeh know.

JOSIE. A couple of large bottles 'd go down well now.

BREDA *enters*.

BREDA. There y'are, Josie, I got those few things for yeh. (*Soap, face cloth, toothpaste, etc.*)

JOSIE. Oh right. Thanks Breda. Did yeh have enough?

BREDA. Yeah.

RORY. He has poor Breda runnin' around the place for him.

BREDA. Shut up you, and leave him alone.

RORY. Oh lord! Stop!

BREDA. God help him.

TED *returns*. JOSIE *opens up his overnight bag and puts the stuff into it.*

RORY. Do yeh know that Ted?

TED. What?

RORY. You and me don't know nothin' about women compared to this fella . . . What did yeh think of Downtown Munich last night, Breda? Queer bad weren't they?

BREDA. Oh they were alright. Sure they're only a crowd of young lads, anyway.

RORY. Yeah well, one of them became old before his time last night then, I don't mind tellin' yeh.

BREDA. Here listen, yeh know what you'll do – seein' as how we won't have Josie with us for a little while. Sing us that new song that yeh sang last night.

RORY. What?

BREDA. Go ahead . . . Wait 'til I make sure that . . . (*She goes to the door and looks across the street*.) No, I'm alright. Go on. Whatdoyoucallit . . . Sayonara Street!

RORY. Sayonara Street?

BREDA. Yeah.

RORY (*looking at his watch*). Breda!

BREDA. Never mind about that. Go ahead.

RORY. Huh?

BREDA. Go on out of that.

RORY. Is this one for real, or what, lads?

TERRY. What? I'm sure Josie is in no form for singin' now, and he just about to go into the hospital.

JOSIE. God I don't mind at all, I'll sing alright.

RORY *and* TERRY *look at one another in amazement.*

RORY. Alright, you're the boss . . . Come on, Ted. get your ass out here. (RORY *rolls back the sheet from the piano.*)

TERRY. Jaysus, if anyone sees us singin' at this hour of the day, we'll be all certified, that's all.

RORY. Not at all.

TERRY. Close over that auld door there then Rory, will yeh.

RORY. Right . . . Come on Ted, will yeh

RORY *closes the door.* TED *comes away from the window and over to the piano.*

TED. What are we doin'? Sayonara?

TERRY. Yeah.

RORY (*to* JOSIE *while he makes a face behind* TERRY'*s back*). You make sure yeh open up your lungs boy.

JOSIE. Come on, will yez.

SONG. Here We Are
It's Sayonara Street
We've Come This Far
And Now We Are Complete
It's Sayonara Street
Goodbye.

Here We Go
I Guess This Is The End
Which Only Goes To Show
That We Were More Than Friends
You see.

Change.

On Sayonara Street
You Know You're Alive
You're Gazing At Your Feet
With Tears In Yours Eyes.

Here We Are
It's Sayonara Street
We're Come This Far
And Now We Are Complete
It's Sayonara Street
Goodbye.

BREDA *applauds. Then she rises and goes across to give* JOSIE *a hug.*

BREDA. I'll see yeh, Josie. Look after yourself now hon, won't yeh? And listen, don't worry about it. It'll be alright.

JOSIE. Yeah, right Breda. And thanks for gettin' us the things.

BREDA. You're welcome. Have yeh a lift up to the hospital and all, yeah?

JOSIE. Yeah. Rory is givin' us a run up like, yeh know.

BREDA. Oh right. You look after him now. do yeh hear me?

RORY. Yeah right, Breda.

BREDA. And stay with him until he's checked in and all . . . I'll come up and see yeh as soon as you're done. I'd better run meself, or I'll be shot. I'll see yeh, Josie.

JOSIE. Yeah, see yeh Breda.

BREDA (*going*). Bye lads.

TERRY. All the best, Breda.

TED. Good luck, Breda.

RORY. See yeh, Breda.

BREDA *is gone. A slight sad pause.*

RORY (*going for his jacket*). I left the car in the chapel yard, Josie. I'll go and bring it around – save yeh . . .

JOSIE *is watching* TERRY, *who is going about his work.*

JOSIE. Huh? . . . Yeah, I want to go over and get an auld paper meself.

RORY. We never lost it all the same though lads, did we? Hah?

He chuckles sadly. JOSIE *looks at the others, smiles and they leave.* TED, *who is still sitting at the piano, turns to watch him go.* TERRY *is watching* TED *all the time.*

TED. What?

TERRY. I know you've been seein' her, Ted.

TED. What?

TERRY. You're some sly boy! Yeh never said nothin' about it, or anythin'.

TED. Yeah well, it's hardly somethin' a fella 'd want to blab about now, is it? I mean to say . . . How did yeh find out about it, anyway?

TERRY. She told me herself that she was seein' someone. I've just put two and two together now.

TED. She told yeh.

TERRY. Yeah Ted, she told me . . . I had a feelin' there was somethin' on your mind this while back.

TED. Yeah? . . . And would yeh say Rory suspects anythin'?

TERRY. Rory? Why should Rory. . . Oh shit!

TED. What?

TERRY. Do you mean to tell me that you've been knockin' around with Rory's missus.

TED. Yeah. Why, who did you think it was?

TERRY. It don't matter . . . How long has this been goin' on?

TED. It started the night I went up to start the presses for her. She came over to me and . . . Well one thing led to another like, yeh know.

TERRY. How far has it gone?

TED. All the way. She's goin' to tell him tonight or tomorrow mornin' I think.

TERRY. Tell him! What does she want to tell him for? I mean what he don't know won't hurt him, will it? This'll all just blow over, and there be no real harm done. Say nothin', I say. It wasn't right what yeh done but . . . Well I mean to say, these things happen like, yeh know. Two people get thrown together like that. Well, it's only natural, ain't it?

TED. It's not goin' to blow over, Terry. I've asked her to move in with me.

TERRY. Yeh what? Are yeh mad or somethin'? Yeh can't do that.

TED. Why not?

TERRY. He's your best fuckin' friend, for fuck's sake.

TED. That don't come into it, Terry.

TERRY. Your best friend don't come into it?

TED. You don't understand, Terry. I mean to say this is not just a quick whatdoyoucallit or anythin'. I got her under my skin, yeh know – right where it hurts. When she's not around I keep wonderin' where she is and when I'm with her I don't want it to end. Yeh know. I mean what can I do?

TERRY. What can yeh do! I'll tell yeh what yeh can, Ted. Yeh can try and . . .

TED. I mean to say I've been worried sick about all of this like, yeh know . . . And I did try to stay away from her for a while and all but . . . I don't know . . .

TERRY. Don't do it, Ted. Don't do it to him. Please. You'll never have any luck if yeh do this kind of thing to your friends. Yeh know. I'm serious, Ted.

TED. Yeah well, unfortunately, so am I.

TERRY. What?

TED. Look, I don't want to be here when Rory gets back. I've been offered a bit of a tangle down the road there. I'm goin' to take my tools with me.

TERRY. What? (TERRY *watches* TED *gather up his tools*.) . . . Yeah, right Ted, you do that. Jesus! . . . (TERRY *paces up and down*.) . . . Oh Lord , Jaysus Ted! . . . Ted, Ted, Ted!

JOSIE *is standing in the doorway now*.

TED. I'll see yeh, Josie. Good luck in the hospital.

JOSIE. Yeah, see yeh Ted.

TED *takes a last look around and leaves*.

He told yeh, then?

TERRY. Can you believe that? Can yeh fuckin' well believe that? And they're supposed to be best friends.

JOSIE. Not any more, they ain't.

TERRY. Poor Rory'll be devastated about this though, yeh know. It'll break his heart, so it will.

JOSIE. Ah well, that's what friends are for, I suppose.

TERRY. Hah? . . . This 'll put the kybosh on The Cavalcaders for a while too won't it? Between one thing and another, I mean.

JOSIE. I suppose.

TERRY. It's all comin' apart Josie, I think. It's all fallin' apart boy! I wouldn't mind, but I promised poor auld Eamon that I'd try and keep it all together, yeh know. But it's queer hard sometimes though, yeh know.

JOSIE. I know.

Slight pause.

TERRY. So when do yeh think they'll do yeh, then?

JOSIE. I don't know. In the mornin', I hope.

TERRY. But sure I'll come up and see yeh tonight, so. Make sure you're settled in and that..

JOSIE. Right. Don't forget me grapes.

TERRY. Yeah right. And I'll bring yeh up a couple of good cowboy books too – keep yeh off the nurses.

Slight pause.

JOSIE. I'll see yeh then, Terry.

TERRY. Yeah, see yeh, me auld mate. Good luck . . .

JOSIE *exits. Pause. Lights down. Lights rise on the shop. Night has fallen.* TERRY *is alone. There is a rap on the window.* TERRY *goes across to open the door. He is surprised to find* BREDA *standing there. He invites her in.*

BREDA. Did yeh get up to see Josie after?

TERRY. Yeah, I went up to see him this evenin'.

BREDA. Well, did he settle in alright, yeah?

TERRY. Yeah, he's in right form up there. Yeh should see the state of the big pyjamas on him.

BREDA. When are they doin' him?

TERRY. In the mornin', I think. Oh he'll be grand . There's a fella who don't look so hot, mind yeh – he's in the bed opposite Josie there – whatshisname, the one legged man from The Faythe. He was an insurance man.

BREDA. Oh poor Mister Kelly.

TERRY. Yeah. They had to amputate his other leg, yeh know.

BREDA. Oh God! . . . Jaysus, you'd only think you'd be bad, wouldn't yeh?

TERRY. Yeah . . .

Slight pause. TERRY *goes to her, kisses her tenderly, touches her face and hair and tries to take her in his arms. She resists, pushing him away gently.*

BREDA. Whoo . . . That's not why I'm here.

TERRY. No? . . . Sorry!

BREDA *chuckles and touches his face.*

BREDA. It's been so long since I touched yeh . . . Have yeh finished with that young one yet?

TERRY. What young one?

BREDA *throws him a dirty look.*

Oh! . . . Yeah – looks like it.

BREDA. Good.

TERRY. Is it? For who?

BREDA. For you.

> TERRY *laughs*. BREDA *moves away from him*.

TERRY. Have you been seein' anyone else since?

BREDA. No . . . You're delighted, ain't yeh?

TERRY. It makes no odds to me.

BREDA. Get out of it, you'd die if yeh ever heard of me goin'
with someone else. Yeh would though, Terry. That's the
difference between you and me, yeh see. I don't care who
you've been with before or since, as long as I end up with your
name engraved on me locket. Even if yeh do write songs about
other women!

TERRY. What?

BREDA. Did You See That Girl! . . . That's the first thing I'd have
to do if I got yeh – run that bloody bank clerk out of town.

TERRY. That song wasn't written about her.

BREDA. Oh yeah, pull the other one Terry.

TERRY. I'm tellin' yeh it wasn't. It was about you. (BREDA
scoffs.) . . . I'm tellin' yeh . . . I was here all by meself right,
tryin' to think of somethin' to write about. I went to the
window – half hopin' I'll admit to see Beautiful Bundoran
goin' by but there was no sign of her. Anyway the next thing
you came out of the hairdressers and I saw yeh goin' down the
street, with your little slender neck on yeh and all, and your
raincoat clingin' into your body when yeh walked. And then
yeh said hello to someone, and I knew straight away that this
street belonged to you, that no one else could compare to yeh –
not around here anyway. So I wrote the song.

He sings softly.)

. . . Hey Mister. Did You See That Girl. She Walks Around
Like She Owned The World. You'd Think She Owned The
World . . .

BREDA. Yeh always were a lovely liar, Terry.

TERRY. Huh?

BREDA. What's wrong with yeh, Terry?

TERRY. How do yeh mean?

BREDA. Well, you're goin' around the place there – I don't know
– runnin' away all the time. I mean what the hell's wrong with
yeh at all, eh? Yox're 'ike a fella who's just waitin' for
somethin' better to come along or somethin'. Nothin' better is
goin' to come along Terry. I'm the best you're goin' to do boy!
Resign yourself to it! (*He chuckles*.) . . . I mean what is it
you're supposed to be waitin' for anyway?

TERRY. Oh I don't know Breda. . . . Sometimes I think I'm just
waitin' for him to come back and tell me that he's sorry or
somethin', yeh know. Childish I know but there yeh go . . .
I always knew that he'd take her from me, yeh know –
eventually. Well I always knew he could if he wanted to, let's
put it that way . . . I never had any peace with her. Right from
the word go. I was always wonderin' where she was and who
she was with, and what she was up to, and all the rest of it.
I mean it wasn't all Rogan's fault or anythin'. Not really! . . .
Then one rainy Sunday afternoon shortly after we were married
she went missin' for a few hours. I nearly went frantic lookin'
for her – down the auld side streets and alleyways I went –
walkin' around for hours in the rain. Nearly drove meself
doolally I did . . . I went home then only to discover that she
was already there before me – the table set , the tea ready.
She'd been to her mother's. I could have kicked meself. Until I
saw her pluck a bit of moss from the hem of her dress.

Silence.

BREDA. He was never a patch on you, Terry.

TERRY. Yeah, that's why he ended up with the rose and me with
the thorn.

BREDA. Thanks very much.

TERRY. What? (*He chuckles sadly and touches her hand
tenderly.*) I never knew you fancied Jacques?

BREDA. The other way round, yeh mean.

TERRY. Yeah?

BREDA. Don't sound so surprised Terry. It could happen, yeh
know.

He laughs.

BREDA. I used to love lookin' at you, yeh know. I used to make
plans to kidnap yeh and everything . . . I'd give anything to be
able to turn back the clock for yeh, Terry. To turn yeh back into
the lovely fella yeh used to be that time . . . Where did he go to at
all, eh?

She touches his face, kisses him gently and leaves. Lights down.

Lights rise. TERRY *is dressed in his . . avy overcoat.* RORY. *enters from the back room and goes behind the counter to put the kettle on.*

RORY. We'll have a cup of tea I think . . . Are yeh alright, Terry?

TERRY. Yeah. A bit hot, that's all.

RORY. What? Jaysus you're boilin' up there. Are yeh OK?

TERRY. Yeah, I'm alright.

RORY *bends down and picks up a cardboard box full of stuff from the floor – old newspapers and photographs, etc. He puts it on the counter.*

RORY. There's a feckin' rake of stuf. nere, yeh know. All the auld music sheets though, hah? And Eamon's auld tunin' fork.

TERRY. What?

RORY. Look at this! . . . *(Reading from an old newspaper.)* FREAK STORM ROCKS THE WOODENWORKS. 'A freak storm rocked the Woodenworks and devastated the quayside last Friday night when heavy waves pounded the waterfront and the surrounding area.' Look at the size of those waves, Terry. That's a great picture ain't it? Hah? *(He finds an old newspaper cutting.)* YOUNG WOMAN PLUNGES TO HER DEATH! 'A young woman plunged from the bridge into the water last Friday night. Eye witnesses said that they could hear the young woman cry out for help before she hit the water but the high winds and heavy seas hampered her rescue and she was tragically drowned . . . That was the queer one who used to work over in the little corner shop here, Terry. I heard after that she was knockin' around with your man Poe the undertaker, yeh know. They say she was pregnant for him and he dumped her. And he a Confraternity man too, hah! *(He chuckles.)* . . . Jaysus she got an awful death after. the poor crator anyway!

NUALA *appears in he back room doorway and there is somethi . . . . bout her appearance.* TERRY *turns to look . . . . isible to* RORY *throughout the scene.*

But s. . . . . sn't right in the head anyway like, yeh know. She was a bit airy I think, wasn't she?

NUALA *comes towards* TERRY.

NUALA. He's alrig . . . there, of course . . . With his black suit and his big black coat and is pioneer badge and his fáinne and his black diamond on is arm and all the rest of it. Well maybe he won't feel so tall when I spill the beans on him. Maybe he won't look so sure of himself then.

TERRY. You say nothin'. That man is a married man with a family.

NUALA. So?

TERRY. You knew that before yeh started foolin' around with him. Now take your punishment and stop whingin'.

NUALA. So I'm the one who has to pay the piper while he gets away scot free is that it?

TERRY. Are you on somethin', or what?

NUALA. What?

TERRY. Did you take somethin'? Nuala, did you take somethin', I said.

NUALA. Yeah. A spoonful of sugar . . . (*She laughs.*)

TERRY. What?

NUALA. I think I'm in trouble, Terry.

TERRY. What do yeh mean?

NUALA. And there's an auld fog comin' down around me too, yeh know.

TERRY. What do yeh mean, you're in trouble?

NUALA. Sometimes I find meself lookin' into a sort of a two-way mirror. I'm sort of on the inside, yeh know – lookin' out at meself.

TERRY. Nuala, what do yeh mean, you're in trouble?

NUALA. Sometimes I look into the mirror and there's no reflection there at all. No shadow either. I go around the place lookin' behind me all the time lookin' for a shadow. It's as if I don't really exist at all, yeh know . . . He used to beat me, yeh know. With his belt. Down in the cellar below his shop. Do you think I bring out the worst in men, Terry? (*She smiles manically.*)

TERRY. What?

NUALA. He told me I was like Eve. He said that Eve came into the Garden and ruined everything. Take me back Terry, please. Let's start again . . .

TERRY. No way.

NUALA. It's a terrible lousy thing to do, yeh know Terry – to take somebody's love and throw it back in their face like that.

TERRY. I never took your love.

NUALA. It's a queer lousy thing to do boy.

TERRY. I never took your love. I never said anythin' about love.

NUALA. If you don't take me back I swear I'll throw meself off of the bridge or somethin'.

TERRY. Now don't start that, Nuala. Yeh know that kind of talk gets on my wick. Anyway you made your bed the night yeh chose him instead of me.

NUALA. You told me to.

TERRY. I what?

NUALA. You said you were only usin' me. You told me to.

TERRY. I told yeh to! Get the fuck out of here, will yeh! I told yeh to!

NUALA falls to her knees and wraps her arms around TERRY's legs, clinging to him in desperation.

NUALA. Please Terry, take me back. I promise yeh I'll do anythin' yeh want. I swear . . .

TERRY. Come up out of it, will yeh. Stop haulin' out of me! Come up I said. Stand up. Get up. Look at yeh. Look, there's your shadow there behind yeh. And there's mine. Yours is young and mine is old. I'm old and you're young. Get it? Got it? Good! Now hold on to it.

NUALA. If you don't take me back I'm goin' to throw meself off the bridge, yeh know.

TERRY. Throw yourself off the bridge! You wouldn't have the nerve to throw yourself off that counter there. Yeh haven't even got the guts to look at yourself in the mirror, let alone throw yourself off the bridge.

NUALA. I will. I'll do it. I'll show the lot of yeh. I'll show you. I'll show him too. Because you're nothin' only a pair of lousers, Terry. Dirty lousers yeh are, the pair of yeh. (*She is backing her way towards the door.*)

TERRY. Nuala.

NUALA. It's a terrible lousy thing to do, yeh know . I mean to say yeh take somebody's love and throw it back in their face like that . . . I'll do it. I swear to God, I'll do it . . .

TERRY. Nuala.

She turns and flees.

Nuala . . .

TED and JOSIE enter from the back room in high spirits. TED goes to the piano and they launch into 'Genevieve', barber shop style.

TERRY. Nuala . . . Nuala . . . Nuala . . .

> TERRY *turns to find* TED *sitting at the piano.* RORY *is at his side.* JOSIE *is in his usual place, sitting on the edge of the piano.* TED *and* JOSIE *are in their stage suits. They have drifted into, 'Now Is The Hour'.* TERRY'*s face lights up at the sight and sound of them. He joins in with the singing, his hands outstretched.*

RORY. Hey Terry, these two fellas wore their suits into the pub, yeh know.

SONG. Soon I'll Return To Find
You Waiting Here . . .

TERRY. Oon the lads. All me auld mates, hah.

> TED *goes into a 'I Say I Say I Say' routine on the piano.*

JOSIE. I say I say I say. Did you hear about the man who tried to poison his wife with a razor blade. He gave her arse an nick.

RORY. I say I say I say. Did you hear about the three hens?

JOSIE and TERRY. The Three Hens?

RORY. Yes, the Three Hens. One was normal, one was dyslexic and the third was a nymphomaniac. The first one said 'cocka doodle doo,' the second said ,'doodle doodle cock', and the third said, 'any cock'll doo.'

JOSIE and TERRY (*sing*). I am a Westmeath Bachelor and my age is twenty-three.

TERRY. I say I say I say. Any news on the budget?

JOSIE. The budget? Ah yes, I do believe that aeroplanes are going up, submarines are going down, while envelopes and notepaper remain stationary.

ALL (*sing*) And That's Why I'm A Bachelor And I Don't Intend To Wed.

> *They laugh.*

TED. Did yeh see the state of the auld caretaker when he heard us doin' the 'any cock'll do' joke. He nearly jawlocked himself laughin', that's all.

RORY. And did yeh see the big bunch of keys he had on him? It's a wonder he didn't do himself a mischief liftin' them.

JOSIE. Yeah, some dirty get laced the poor man's tea with whisky too, though.

RORY. Yeah I wonder who that was now?

JOSIE. Hey boy, don't look at me.

TED. Did yeh see him goin' down the stairs. He was like a puppet. Happy New Year says he!

JOSIE (*tearful with laughter*). He was absolutely footless wasn't he? Oh dear, oh dear . . .

TERRY. All the boys, hah! And Josie, me auld mate!

JOSIE. What . . . (JOSIE's *expression changes as they embrace.*) Your uncle Eamon knows, Terry. She's after tellin' him I think.

TERRY. What?

JOSIE. He knows. She told him.

TERRY. When?

JOSIE. She told him, I'm tellin' yeh . . . (JOSIE *breaks away, turns to* TED *and* RORY.) . . . Yeah, Eamon's missus. She took the pair of us on in the back room there.

RORY. Yeah?

JOSIE. We were only young fellas at the time now. I mean to say, we didn't know any better or anythin'. But she was lyin' up on the auld table inside there. Terry went into her first and then when he came out, she called me in.

RORY. Jaysus she must have been mad for it, was she?

JOSIE. Oh stop! Although she was sort of cryin' when I went in though, like, yeh know.

RORY. Yeah? . . . Jaysus hah!

TED *begins to play The Alleluia from Eamon's mass.*

TERRY. Are yeh sure she told him Josie? Where's me uncle now, Josie? . . . Josie . . . Jesus . . .

BREDA (*enters*). Are you fellas comin' over to the dance, or what?

TED. What? Yeah right Breda.

JOSIE. New Year's Eve, Breda, 1968!

BREDA. What about it?

JOSIE. Jacques LePouvier kissed Marian Noakes and what happened?

BREDA. I don't know, tell me, what happened?

JOSIE. She blossomed! Right or wrong? And this was a one with neither shape nor make to her now. New Year's Eve, right. Jacques goes over, takes her in his arms and boom. Her whole face lit up, boy I'm not coddin' yeh. Two weeks later Dinky Doyle is tellin' me that he's after fallin' in love with her – a girl he wouldn't even look at the summer before. Marvellous too what can happen though, ain't it? Hah? The face of Breda!

BREDA. The face of you, yeh mean!

JOSIE. What?

BREDA. Go away from me, will yeh, and come on.

JOSIE. What?

> BREDA *leaves. The others make to follow.* JOSIE *laughs, eyes to heaven.*

Oh Marian Noakes, where are yeh now?

The others laugh. TED *and* JOSIE *leave.* TERRY *stands to watch them go. A choir is singing the Alleluia, heard only by* TERRY. *He basks in it, tears in his eyes.* RORY *comes up behind him.*

RORY. Are yeh alright, Terry?

TERRY. What? Yeah.

RORY. The only thing is worryin' me now is how the hell we're goin' to get this auld piano out the door here. I mean I know technically speaking if it went in, then it should come out. But how? . . . How did they get it in here, anyway?

TERRY. What? The piano?

RORY. Yeah.

TERRY. They had an awful job, sure. The whole street was out pushin' and shovin'. And that came out of our little kitchen, yeh know. An awful weight in it, too. In the end they had to take down the doorframe and everything and big Tom Nail the coalman told everyone to stand aside while he pushed it through sideways through the hole in the wall. Meself and Josie were only little lads that time and I was killed tryin' to look inside the piano because someone told me that there was a man's name carved under the lid somewhere It was great to hear Eamon's Mass sung at Josie's funeral that time though, wasn't it?

RORY. What?

TERRY. Josie's brother asked me to sit in with the family, yeh know It was queer nice of him boy! And later on I helped to carry the coffin with them. Poor auld Josie though hah! . . . A spoonful of sugar, says she!

RORY. Who? (TERRY *looks at him vacantly.*)

> RORY *looks at* TERRY, *a little concerned about him. He goes across to the counter. He leafs through an old dusty child's*

copy book which he leaves on the counter. He picks up an old photograph.

There's a great photo. Who is it? There's you, anyway. And Josie. Josie didn't change a bit did he? And who's that lad? . . . He looks like Billy Fury, don't he?

TERRY. What?

TERRY *looks at the photo.* RORY *goes back to the counter for the box.*

RORY. I'll leave this auld box over the bench for yeh, Terry, just in case you're wanting anything out of it or anything.

TERRY. Yeah, right, Rory. Thanks.

RORY. I'm goin' to tell yeh one thing though, me auld son, but you're one sound man boy!

TERRY. What? . . . I've done some queer things in me time though Rory, yeh know. I mean I 've a lot to answer for .

RORY. Show me the man that hasn 't.

RORY *lays the cardboard down on the bench and goes back in behind the counter.* TERRY *sits on the bench and takes from the box a sprig of mistletoe. He titters.*

RORY. What?

TERRY. Mistletoe, be Jaysus!

RORY. What? Yeah.

TERRY *loses himself in thought. We hear music far off in the distance, a corny band playing The Conga.* RORY *is oblivious to it until* JOSIE *and* BREDA *and* TED *and* NUALA *come dancing in with party hats on their heads,*

JOSIE. Happy New Year! . . . (*To* TERRY.) Happy New Year, me auld son.

BREDA (*breaks away to kiss him*). Happy New Year, Terry.

TERRY'*s face is aglow as they all dance into the back room and back out again,* RORY *joining them.*

JOSIE. Happy New Year!

JOSIE *snakes them in behind the counter and then back into the back room again,* NUALA *staying behind, a little breathless.*

NUALA. I'm Nuala. I work in the shop across the street.

TERRY. I know. I often saw yeh goin' in and out. I'm Terry .

NUALA. Happy New Year, Terry.

TERRY. The same to you.

NUALA *smiles and eyes the mistletoe in his hand.*

It's a shame to waste it.

NUALA. What?

TERRY goes to her and kisses her gently. She looks into his eyes and sighs. He kisses her again and she responds to him. He touches her face and studies it etc as she basks in the nearness of him.

NUALA (*cooing beneath his touch*). Mmn . . .

The others return. TERRY and NUALA break away from one another. BREDA, full of festive glee, dances with JOSIE through the shop and out onto the street.

TED. What do yeh mean? We go every year ,don't we?

RORY. Not this year, I 'm afraid.

TED. Why not?

RORY. Because Ursula is up in the house on her own with the baby and . . .

TED. Ursula, Ursula,Ursula! You'd give anyone the shits talkin' about Ursula.

RORY. What's that supposed to mean?

TED. Ah.

RORY. I mean it's alright for you, Ted.

TED. Why, because I'm not tied to the apron strings, yeh mean.

RORY. No, because you re nothin', only a lonely bottle with no one belongin' to yeh.

TED. I have plenty of fella to drink with, mate. And I can get a woman anytime I feel like it.

RORY. Yeah sure.

TED. What do yeh mean, yeah sure.

RORY. Yeah sure – yeh can get a woman anytime yeh feel like it.

TED. What?

JOSIE (*returns*). What's wrong with the two of you, eh?

TED (*exits*). He's makin' out.

RORY (*off*). Makin' out? What am I supposed to be makin' out?

TED (*off*). You're makin' out that I'm a whatdoyoucallit . . .

RORY (*off*). Will you go and cop on to yourself Ted . . .

NUALA. I can see yeh workin' from my window, yeh know.

TERRY. Can yeh?

NUALA. Yeah. And the other day I heard yeh singin'.

TERRY. What was I singin'?

NUALA. I don't know. Somethin' about the moon.

TERRY. Somethin' about the moon? It could have been anythin'.

NUALA. I know.

TERRY *chuckles and kisses her again.* JOSIE *turns to look at them.*

JOSIE. Your uncle Eamon's in a pretty bad way over there, Terry. I think maybe you should go over to him . . . Terry.

TERRY (*entranced by the girl*). What?

JOSIE. I say I think maybe you should go over to him. I think she's after tellin' him, yeh know.

TERRY. Yeah.

BREDA (*entering*). Josie, come out here quick will yeh, before these two fellas kill one another out here.

JOSIE. What? What's up?

BREDA. Come on, they're killin' one another out here. (JOSIE *goes*.) . . . They should be ashamed of themselves, two friends fightin' like that on New Year's Eve . . . Are you comin' back to the dance or what Nuala?

NUALA. What? Yeah . . . Are you comin' over?

TERRY. I'll be over in a minute.

NUALA *smiles and follows* BREDA *out the door.*

Music dies. TERRY *chuckles to himself.* RORY *enters from the back room. The music in the distance fades to nothing.*

RORY. What?

TERRY. Nothin'.

RORY. Terry smilin' away to himself there . . . Did yeh see the cups anyway? . . . the place is in an uproar boy . . . When the sheets are shorter the beds look longer, hah! I don't know!

RORY *takes two dusty mugs and goes out to the back room again.* TERRY *tosses the sprig of mistletoe into the box again. He sits. Suddenly* JOSIE *appears in the doorway again, a party hat on his head.*

JOSIE. She's after tellin' him alright. Terry.

TERRY. What? When?

JOSIE. At the stroke of midnight. She's some bitch, boy! Poor auld Eamon is in an awful way over there!

TERRY. Why though? I mean it was so long ago!

NUALA is standing in the back room doorway, laughing. TERRY turns to her.

What?

NUALA. It was probably the first and last time for Josie.

TERRY laughs. He turns to find that JOSIE is gone and then turns to discover that BREDA is standing where NUALA used to be. He frowns and begins pacing the room.

BREDA. I was only dancin' with him, Terry.

TERRY. Yeh danced nearly every second dance with him, is what I heard.

BREDA. Yeah well, that 's why I go down there like – to dance. It's Ballroom Dancin' like, yeh know, and he's sort of my partner . He's a good dancer .

TERRY. I thought Dinky was supposed to be your partner?

BREDA. We changed round. Your man Poe is sort of my partner now.

TERRY. What way did he hold yeh?

BREDA. What? Normal.

TERRY. Show me.

BREDA. He sort of held me like this . . .

TERRY. Show me, I said .

BREDA. What? . . . (*She takes TERRY's arm and guides it around her body.*) . . . He put one arm around me like that and he held my hand in his like that. Yeh know. Just normal!

TERRY. Are yeh sure it wasn't like this?

He draws her roughly towards him. Disappointed, she frees herself from his grip. Pause. He begins to pace again, slightly angry.

How did Josie get on?

BREDA. Good. He sounds good, yeh know – with the orchestra behind him and all. He looks good too . . . But sure you should come down there some night, Terry. You're a lovely dancer.

And it's a right bit of laugh, yeh know. That's all it is Terry – a bit of laugh!

TERRY. Yeah?

He looks at her, full of uncertainty. She nods sadly.

BREDA. . . . . What's wrong with yeh?

TERRY. I don't know. I'm beginnin' to care about where yeh go and who you're with, and all the rest of it. I don't like it.

BREDA. But sure that's good ain't it? That yeh care!

TERRY. I'm not so sure about that.

Slight pause.

BREDA. Yeah well, that's not why I'm here anyway. I need to talk to yeh about somethin' else.

TERRY. What?

She throws him a dirty look.

BREDA. I'm gettin' tired of it Terry – all this cloak and dagger stuff. I mean I'm tired sneakin' round in the dark all the time, yeh know. I want it all out in the open now.

TERRY. How do yeh mean?

BREDA. It's time we settled down Terry – you and me. Yeh know. I mean . . . Don't yeh think it's time we settled down?

TERRY. I've been down that road once before, Breda.

BREDA. Not with me, yeh haven't.

TERRY. No one was supposed to fall, Breda. We agreed. No strings attached . That's what we said.

BREDA. You said, yeh mean.

TERRY. But sure I thought yeh said yeh liked comin' over here anyway? . . . So what is this, an ultimatum or somethin'?

BREDA. Call it what yeh like. But I'm not comin' over here again – not like this anyway. If you want to see me again you can call over to the house for me. Ask me out properly – on a proper date. Take me somewhere nice.

TERRY(*pacing*). Jesus!

BREDA. Will yeh do that for me?

TERRY. I don't know, we'll see.

BREDA (*disappointed*). Oh!

TERRY. Now don't get all stroppy on me. We'll see, I said. Yeh know . . . I mean . . . We'll see.

BREDA. OK. . . . I'll see yeh then, Terry.

TERRY. Yeah right Breda, see yeh.

BREDA *turns to leave. She stops in the doorway to look at him.*

BREDA. Jaysus, Terry!

Slight pause. She leaves sadly. The sound of music as JOSIE appears, dressed in a beautiful white dinner jacket etc. He looks really handsome. He steps up to a microphone and sings, 'Smoke Gets In Your Eyes'. NUALA is standing in the back room doorway, smiling. TERRY looks at her tenderly. He goes to her and takes her in his arms. They dance. They continue to dance when the song ends, their dancing feet shuffling like a played out record. JOSIE is gone.

NUALA. Breda wants me to go Ballroom Dancing with her, yeh know.

TERRY. Does she?

NUALA. Yeah. Do yeh think I should?

TERRY. If yeh like .

NUALA. Would yeh mind?

TERRY *shakes his head.* NUALA *smiles at him tenderly.*

Listen, I'm wantin' you to come over and see my little room sometime . . . Will yeh?

TERRY. OK.

NUALA. I'll read yeh some of my poetry by candlelight. And I'll light a big fire and we'll lie down on the mat together. Will yeh come over though? (TERRY *nods.*) . . . When?

TERRY. Soon.

NUALA. That's good. You'd better, now. I love being with you, Terry, yeh know. I swear the whole world stops turnin' when you're inside of me. And everything goes real quiet. So so silent! All I can hear is the sound of my heart beatin'. And the sound of my own . . . ecstasy . . . I love hearin' about your exploits with all those other women too – where yeh took them and how it all came about and that. Sometimes I pretend to be standin' in their shoes as they come to you. Other times I imagine I'm you waitin' for them to come to me. Like the one about your lovely neighbour with the big bottom who rides her bike past your house every day. And when she came to sell you a raffle ticket or something you asked her in and yeh stripped her naked in the parlour, and yeh told her to stand up on a chair so that you could have a good look at her, and that. I love hearin' that one . . . (TERRY *laughs*.) What?

TERRY. I only made that one up.

NUALA. Yeh what? Yeh didn't . . . Ah yeh didn't . . . That's my favourite one!

TERRY. I know.

NUALA. Yeh didn't though really, did yeh . . . Ah no, that's not fair. (*She hits him playfully.*)

TERRY. What?

NUALA. How many of the others did yeh make up?

TERRY. Hah?

NUALA. I bet yeh made them all up. You were probably never with another woman in your life.

TERRY. Hey. (*He presents himself.*)

She laughs and kisses him. He draws her in close to him.

NUALA. Yes Terry. Yes. Yes . . .

TERRY. We can't. The boys'll be arrivin' soon.

NUALA. Get rid of them.

TERRY. What?

NUALA. Lock the door. Draw the blinds. Turn out the lights.

TERRY. We can't. Yeh know we can't . . . Anyway I'm all washed out.

NUALA. What –

TERRY. I'm bet. You win.

NUALA. Do yeh give up?

TERRY. Yeah. I give up.

She chuckles and looks deep into his eyes.

NUALA. They say you can fall in love with anybody, yeh know. All yeh need is time. But I don't believe that. I believe in fate. And destiny. I believe that you end up where you belong . . . I hope so anyway . . . (*She frowns.*)

TERRY. What's wrong?

NUALA. Sometimes I feel a bit ashamed of the things I ask you to do to me.

TERRY. Why?

NUALA. I don't know. I just do.

TERRY. There's no need to be.

NUALA. I know but . . .

TERRY. . . . Look, I told yeh before, I'd do anything yeh want me to do. As long as yeh don't ask me to hurt yeh or anythin'.

NUALA. You'll probably do that anyway Terry – in time.

Slight pause.

TERRY. You'd better be goin', Nuala.

NUALA. OK . . . When will I see you again?

TERRY. Tomorrow sometime.

NUALA. I love you Terry . . . Did yeh hear me?

TERRY *nods.*

TERRY. Go ahead.

NUALA. OK. . . . Bye.

NUALA *leaves softly. Slight pause.* RORY *enters with the washed mugs.*

RORY. Yeh know I'm nearly sure I saw a man's name somewhere inside that auld piano one time . . . Wait 'til I have a look see . . . I believe the other one is pregnant again too, yeh know.

TERRY. Who's that?

RORY. Ursula. I saw herself and Ted goin' by there just the other day. I wasn't talkin' to them or anythin'. I just said hello to them and that..

TERRY. Yeah?

RORY *is on his belly now, looking inside the piano.*

RORY. All water under the bridge now, Terry. I don't know where this is. I'm nearly sure I . . .

JOSIE *enters, dressed in pyjamas and dressing-gown etc.*

JOSIE. How's it goin', me auld son?

TERRY (*rises, delighted*). Josie!

JOSIE. I see poor auld Kelly in there without a leg to stand on, hah!

TERRY. Yeah.

JOSIE. Thanks for the grapes. (TERRY *nods.*) . . . Thanks for the rabbit says she, the soup was gorgeous. Do yeh miss me?

TERRY. Yeah, I do.

JOSIE. Hah? (*He smiles and sings.*) Heart Of My Heart. I Love That Melody. Too Bad We Had To Part. (TERRY *sings along with him, sadly harmonising.*) I Know A Tear Would Glisten. If Once More I Could Listen. To That Gang That Sang. Heart Of My Heart. (*He chuckles.*) . . .

JOSIE. Jaysus it's gas though too, Terry ain't it, when yeh think of it? Hah? . . . I mean you regret somethin' yeh did a long long time ago and here am I sort of ashamed of somethin' I never done at all . . . But she was sort of cryin' when I went into her though, yeh know. I mean the woman was cryin' for Jaysus sake. Yeh know?

Slight pause. He leaves.

RORY. I was right. Here it is here, look. R. Deacon . . . Sounds like a Protestant name don't it? Or Anglo-Irish or somethin'. A whatdoyoucallit – an aristocratic piano tuner hah! -

During the next speech NUALA appears in the back room doorway.

RORY. You can just picture him though, can't yeh? Goin' from town to town. A little hat on his head, his tools in a bag. Like a doctor! And one of those brown shop coats on him. An auld tunin' fork stickin' up out of his top pocket. He probably stayed down in The White Horse Inn or somewhere – rising up every mornin' to try and drum up a bit of business. The Tate School or the Confraternity Band room or somewhere. Or some auld workingman's club maybe. Mister R. Deacon hah! February 1947! (*He chuckles sadly and puts the piano back together etc. NUALA smiles a forgiving smile and leaves. BREDA enters.*) Congratulations Breda!

BREDA. Why, what did I do now?

RORY. You've just inherited a piano.

BREDA. Oh no, that one there?

RORY. Yeah.

BREDA (*to TERRY*). Well it's goin' up in the attic. I'm not havin' that in me livin' room . . . Do yeh hear me? He's been threatenin' to have the attic converted this six months or more and he still hasn't got around to it. Are yeh alright?

RORY. He's burnin' up there, so he is.

BREDA. What? . . . He is too. What's wrong with yeh?

TERRY. I'm not well.

BREDA. Aw! Yeh poor crator yeh. Come on, I'll get yeh home to bed. There's a terrible dose goin' around though, yeh know. He's burnin' up there . . . But sure, I suppose that's way out of tune and everythin', is it?

TERRY. No, it's not too bad, mind yeh. (*He crosses to the piano.*)

BREDA. What? How are things, Rory?

RORY. Alright.

BREDA. Are yeh all set?

RORY. Just about. Yeh won't know the place the next time yeh see it, Breda.

BREDA. Yeah? Big plans hah?

RORY. Oh yeah. New counter along here, a bench out there and bare floorboards out to the door all varnished and all.

BREDA. Lovely. It sounds lovely anyway.

TERRY *is playing, 'One Heart Broken', on the piano.*

RORY. The Cavalcaders, hah! Take a look in that auld cardboard box there, Breda. Your whole life'll flash before yeh girl. (BREDA *goes to the box and plucks from it the old newspaper.*) That's a great picture, Breda, ain't it? Freak Storm Rocks The Woodenworks hah!

BREDA. Mmn . . . That was the night you came knockin' on my door wasn't it? He was afraid of the dark, weren't yeh? (*She goes to him.*)

TERRY (*nods*). That was before I got lucky.

BREDA. Aw! (*She hugs and kisses him.*)

TERRY. How did your dancin' go after?

BREDA. Alright. Little Dinky nearly danced the legs off of me that's all. (*She sings.*) Jealousy. Da Da Da Da Da Da Da . . . Did yeh ever see him dancin', Rory?

RORY. Who's that?

BREDA. Little Dinky Doyle. He's a lovely dancer. I'm tryin' to get this fella to come down but he won't budge at all.

RORY. Why not?

TERRY. I'm bad enough now.

BREDA. It's a right bit of laugh down there though, yeh know. All the auld songs an' all . . .

RORY (*reading from a dusty child's copy book*). Oh Rowan Tree, Oh Rowan Tree, Oh Won't You Tell Me. Why Do the Wind Not Blow Through Your Leaves? And Why Do I Feel So Safe

In Your Breast? Oh Rowan Tree, Oh Rowan Tree, Why Are
You So Blessed?

RORY *shakes his head and chuckles.* TERRY *buries his head
into his hands.*

BREDA. Listen, come on. I'll get you home to bed. I'll see yeh,
Rory.

RORY. Yeah right, lads.

BREDA. And listen, good luck with everything. And don't forget
if yeh ever need anything now, yeh know where we are. Tell
him.

TERRY. Oh sure he knows that. All he has to do is shout.

BREDA. Do yeh hear that?

RORY. Yeah. Thanks very much.

BREDA *gives her little wave.*

TERRY. I'll see yeh in the mornin' sometime, Rory.

BREDA. No yeh won't. You won't be seein' anyone for a few
days – until yeh shake off that auld flu or whatever it is yeh
have.

TERRY. That's what I've to put up with now, Rory.

BREDA. It's a pity about him, Rory, ain't it? Hah? Come on. Bye
hon.

RORY. Yeah, see yeh, lads.

TERRY. I wonder if there's any pictures of Beautiful Bundoran in
that auld box.

BREDA. Come on. I'll Beautiful Bundoran yeh.

TERRY What? I'll see yeh, Rory.

TERRY *winks at* RORY. *They leave. Pause.* RORY *puts the
light out and leaves. Pause. Lights down.*

I'M LEANING ON THE LAMPPOST

ALLELUIA

ONE HEART BROKEN

THAT GIRL

SAYONARA STREET

GENEVIEVE

NOW IS THE HOUR

A Nick Hern Book

The Cavalcaders first published in Great Britain and the
Republic of Ireland in 1994 as a paperback original
by Nick Hern Books, 14 Larden Road, London W3 7ST
in association with the Royal Court Theatre, Sloane Square,
London SW1W 8AS

Typeset by Country Setting, Woodchurch, Kent TN26 3TB
Printed by Cox & Wyman Ltd, Reading, Berks

Front cover photo of the Peacock Theatre production
by Charles Collins

Lines from 'Leaning on a Lamppost' by Noel Gay
reproduced by courtesy of Richard Armitage Ltd,
8/9 Frith Street, London W1V 5TZ

Music from the songs by Billy Roche has been arranged
by Pat Fitzpatrick

A CIP catalogue record for this book is available from the
British Library

ISBN 1-85459-291-2